For Ed—

Best wishes—Have a good
ride with the cavalry—

*[signature]*

10.VII.93

Monroe

# SADDLE SOLDIERS

*The Civil War Correspondence*
*of General William Stokes*
*of the*
*4th South Carolina Cavalry*

by Lloyd Halliburton

Sandlapper Publishing Company, Inc.
Orangeburg, South Carolina

**Sandlapper Publishing Company, Inc.**
Orangeburg, South Carolina

**Library of Congress Cataloging-in-Publication Data**

Stokes, William, 1833–1905.
    Saddle soldiers : the Civil War correspondence of General
William Stokes of the 4th South Carolina Cavalry / [edited]
by Lloyd Halliburton.
        p.    cm.
    Includes bibliographical references and index.
    ISBN 0–87844–115–8 (hardcover : acid-free)
    1. Stokes, William, 1833–1905—Correspondence.
2. Generals—Southern States—Correspondence. 3. United
States—History—Civil War, 1861–1865—Personal narra-
tives, Confederate.  4.  Confederate States of America.
Army. South Carolina Cavalry Regiment—History.
5.  United States—History—Civil War, 1861–1865—
Regimental histories.  6.  South Carolina—History—Civil
War, 1861–1865—Regimental histories.  7.  South Caro-
lina—History—Civil War, 1861–1865—Personal narratives,
Confederate.  I.  Halliburton, Lloyd.  II.  Title.
E467.1.S868A4    1993
973.7'82—dc20                                              93–621
                                                                       CIP

For my great-grandfather,
THORNBURG BERRY HALLIBURTON,
late of Quantrill's Raiders,
and my brother,
Captain THOMAS MICHAEL HALLIBURTON, U.S.A.F.,
who flew combat in Southeast Asia

# CONTENTS

# ACKNOWLEDGEMENTS

This book would have been impossible without its heart. Therefore, my most grateful appreciation is extended to Sunny Stokes French, General Stokes' great-granddaughter, for granting me access to the material in her possession and the permission to publish it.

Additional letters and documents were made available to me by Frank N. Handal, my publisher, the Division of Archives and History, Raleigh, North Carolina, and Allan Stokes of the Caroliniana Library of the University of South Carolina. This collection has enriched the contents of the book immeasurably; they have my gratitude.

The George C. Marshall Research Library made the task pleasant by providing a "clean, well-lighted place" in which I could work during the early phases of writing and peruse the reference collections necessary to accomplish the research. For valuable assistance and courtesy, I would like to mention three of its staff members in particular: Lynn Birabaur, research assistant, who photocopied microfilm for me at the National Archives; Diane Elliot, research assistant, who oriented me to the library's facilities; and Anthony R. Crawford, assistant archivist, whose expertise and advice saved me valuable time.

In any research, money is always an object. The VMI Foundation and Louisiana Tech University provided grants to defray some of these expenses. Their support is hereby formally recognized.

The author is indebted to Robyn Ray for assistance in interpreting certain terms relating to equestrian material; to Dr. George M. Butler for his skill and timely advice on several matters pertaining to the preparation of the manuscript; to Ralph Pierce for his help on maps and place names; and to Nancy Wooten, my editor, for her meticulousness, keen eye, "generalship," and suggestions that really mattered.

Lastly, a special thanks to my youngest son, Lee, whose thoughtfulness and love and encouragement in all things have never been taken for granted.

L. H.
Ruston, Louisiana

# INTRODUCTION

General William Stokes was born on October 20, 1833, the youngest of ten children. His marriage to Eliza Jane Boulware on March 6, 1856, produced fifteen children and formed the backbone of a distinguished line of senior officers who have rendered faithful service to the United States.

Their first child was William Miles whose son, William Miles, Jr., graduated from the Virginia Military Institute in 1921, saw service in World War II as a major general, and later became the acting superintendent of VMI from April 1 through August 1, 1952.

Another son was Marcus B., who graduated from West Point and attained the rank of brigadier general. He had two sons, Marcus B., Jr., also a West Point graduate and retired brigadier general, and John Hall, a 1931 graduate of the Virginia Military Institute and retired Air Force colonel.

General Stokes' great-granddaughter, Sunny Stokes French, made many of the letters and other memorabilia available for this volume. French, herself, is married to Harry W. French, a VMI graduate of the class of 1950B, who retired as a colonel after a distinguished career (three Silver Stars) in the United States Army.

Several years prior to the Civil War, General Stokes, then a captain, had commanded a company of cavalry in the South Carolina State Militia.[1] When the war broke out, he entered the Confederate Army with the same rank from his home in St. Bartholomews Parish[2] near Branchville, South Carolina, on January 16, 1862 (for a period of one year, later changed to the duration of the war), at Smokes Cross Road and saw active service on the South Carolina coast in 1862 and 1863. On May 6, 1862, he was promoted to major of the 2d Battalion which, in August of that year, was incorporated into the 4th Regiment, South Carolina Cavalry. By December 16, 1862, Stokes was promoted to lieutenant colonel[3] and second-in-command under Colonel B. Huger Rutledge. As the letters in this volume clearly show, the appointment as second-in-command was in name only. Colonel Rutledge was away from the Regiment during many of the engagements; the responsibility for command in combat fell to General Stokes.

In the spring of 1864, the Regiment was ordered to join the Army of Northern Virginia. Together with the 5th and 6th South Carolina Cavalry Regiments, it became Butler's Brigade of Hampton's Division, and took part in some of the heaviest fighting of the war: Hawes' Shop, Cold Harbor, Trevilian Station, and in numerous other battles that were connected with the defense of Petersburg and Richmond. In these battles, General Stokes had a right to be proud of the 4th South Carolina Cavalry, for it maintained a reputation of excellence among the fighting men, whose opinion is the only one in war that really counts and which army politics and propaganda cannot create: "Our Brigade has contributed not a little to these favorable results [of the Virginia campaign]," Stokes wrote, "and its merits and fighting qualities are being acknowledged very generally, but the troops that have been here all the time are jealous of us." And in another letter, he quoted an unnamed source: ". . . It is no use to deny it— Butler's Brigade can out fight any troops on foot in the Army of Northern Virginia." The ultimate praise though, was attributed to a captured Union captain: "I hear that they use [sic] not to saddle their horses for the Virginia Cavalry, but since Butler's Brigade got here they had to learn."

Considering the conditions under which he wrote, the letters show General Stokes to be articulate, possessing a vivid memory, cool, and seemingly nonchalant under fire as he underplayed the danger of death by stating the facts as he saw them, omitting descriptions that could reflect on the morbidity of his surroundings. There is a certain eloquence to the sketches which he painted. They do not take on the pretentiousness of "war stories"— exaggerated and laced with the egotism of narcissism or solipsism. Rather, he described war. And the war he fought in was no different from others in that war has always been hell—and the American Civil War was clearly that.

General Stokes, in addition to being a leader of men in combat, showed himself to be a gentleman, the complete human being, capable of error but strong enough of character to endure the reprisal that error brings. Upon returning to his regiment after overstaying a leave, he was placed under arrest and confined to quarters. In spite of this indignity, he displayed little bitterness or resentment while awaiting a court-martial that he believed would exonerate him. Although the details of his absence from duty are never specified—the letters suggest that he remained to resettle his wife in order to remove her from the path of Sherman's march to the sea—he was pardoned by General Robert E. Lee in a general amnesty.

He was no paper god. He was a man whom other men followed, and because of this, because of men who were like him, the South needed no propaganda to indoctrinate or brainwash their men in the field. The cause was visible in the cavalry, expressed in the figures of men on horseback—Hampton, Jackson, Lee—and by boys on foot at New Market, who performed deeds later described in a tapestry of heroism written long after the acrid smell of powder and the stench from the dead had "gone with the wind." It was expressed by the silhouette in the saddle of a man like General Stokes. The expression was that intangible example that today is still known as leadership.

History cannot be erased, even when men try to alter it. The South lost the war; it is true. Today, long-silent cannon merely mark time as their shadows creep across the lawns of innumerable courthouse squares, their grapeshot buried harmlessly in the earth from which the rains of more than a century have washed the blood away. General Stokes and his men can rest easily. They were neither defeated nor destroyed.

It is said, and agreed to by men of integrity, that the ends never justify the means. The writings of General Stokes point out emphatically that the means he espoused—truth, bravery, devotion to duty—certainly did not justify the surrender of the 4th South Carolina Cavalry as the war drew to a close.

As commander of the Regiment at the time of the general surrender near the North Carolina line, General Stokes disbanded it and sent the men home. According to his service record, Stokes himself followed later, bringing with him the headquarters' wagon containing the Regiment's records; however, he awakened one morning to discover that the teamsters and mules that pulled it had disappeared during the night. The personnel records, the fighting heart of the 4th South Carolina Cavalry, were in this wagon. Being unable to move the wagon alone and not wishing to abandon it to scavengers who might come upon it and despoil the only remnants of the Regiment (except what lay in the memories of the survivors), he set fire to it.

In spite of this, the history of the 4th South Carolina Cavalry is basically preserved. The letters and other memorabilia from General Stokes' personal records attest to its accomplishments in the Civil War.

Returning to South Carolina, General Stokes entered politics and was elected to the first State Legislature that was assembled after hostilities. Later, aware of the chaos and injustice that Reconstruction created, he took an active part in the Red Shirt campaign of 1876 that brought his former commander, General Wade Hampton, to the governorship. During the campaign, General Stokes commanded all the clubs of Hampton County. These "clubs" were organizations composed of dismounted riflemen or horsemen armed with sabres. Their purpose was to keep political rallies peaceful and the polls free from corruption. Hampton's motto was "Force without Violence." The clubs saw to it that the motto of that election was more than a string of words. It was a fact.

Upon assuming office, Governor Hampton appointed William Stokes a brigadier general with the task of organizing and eventually commanding the cavalry of Hampton, Beaufort, Colleton, and Charleston counties. As usual, he served faithfully and well.

It is evident that General Stokes was a religious man. Often his letters attribute his safety in battle to the protection of Almighty God. As late as 1903, then in his seventieth year, he was a delegate to the Annual Conference of the South Carolina Methodists, demonstrating that able men continue to lead, even when they deserve to rest.

He died on June 30, 1905, and like Don Quixote, the example shown by the conduct of General Stokes and his men lives after them, in a world marked by the boundaries of idealism, for a cause which they did not betray.

Lloyd Halliburton
The George C. Marshall
Research Library
Lexington, Virginia

# 1861

★ ★ ★

*Throughout the summer of 1861, the State of South Carolina concentrated its war efforts in defense of Charleston and other areas along the coast. Some of these efforts consisted of preparation and assembly of forces sufficient to combat the attack that was expected.*

*The following correspondence to General Stokes, while he was commanding a company in the South Carolina Militia, enumerates some of the administrative duties that were required of him prior to his being called to active service.*

*The letters are published as they were written, with brackets and notes added only to aid understanding. Perhaps because of the conditions under which they were written and also because of changes in style rules over time, the letters sometimes contain punctuation, abbreviations, capitalizations, spellings, grammar, and sentence structure which are inconsistent with traditionally accepted forms of modern American English. To give a true picture of Stokes and the other correspondents, the inconsistencies are left intact. Misspelled proper nouns are noted the first time only.*

Pineville, 5 Sept 1861

Capt

Yours of the 2nd inst. duly recd. I have orders with which form.[ally] to order an election for the vacancy in your Comp[any] on the 4th Saturday in this month. It could not be done on the second Saturday legally.[4] As to the Regt being called out as a whole I am unable to say. It seems that the only troops accepted by the Gov. are those gotten up under the excitement of the moment, and troops that have been organized for years and undergoing the expense and trouble of attending Militia duty at a heavy expense and fatigue have the *go less.* I really don't think it just. If our State are invaded by such a force as that the troops raised under excitement can't drive off then the 4th Regt will be called out whether as a whole or not time will decide. If the State is invaded I shall take the field in some capacity, as a private if the Regt is not ordered out.

I would with pleasure give your brother an appointment as Surgeon or Asst Surgeon, but both offices are filled: the Sur-

3

geon by Dr. T S. Waring & the Asst Surgeon by Dr. Robt. Witsell of Blackville.

Yours very truly

/s/ C. S. Edwards

*Another letter during this early period of the war, from General John E. Tobin, written on September 16, 1861, from Blackville, South Carolina, follows:*

I think it would scarcely be worthwhile to apply for any more arms for your troop. I am sure that my application for you would do no good. Your regular course is to apply to your colonel, to subscribe your requisition there, sign it yourself, and send to me for my signature. But there is no such great demand for arms for Militias, for the war, that it would be useless to apply.

Have you no young men that would like to join my company for the Confederate Service? If you have I should be glad for you to send his name.

Enclosed I send a hand Bill [See Appendix I, No. 3] which please stick up in your Section at [a] conspicuous place.

You say your company is entirely very loyal. I am afraid there are many young men in it now that ought to be in a company for the war. The Governor will never call for your company, nor any other Militia Troop. Your present position will continue to be one of utter inactivity. It is so with all the Militia throughout the State.

If any of you expect to be of any service in this war then train a new "home guard." You will have to connect yourselves with some corps for the Confederate Service.

Yours very truly,

/s/ John E. Tobin

*During these days of little action, Captain Stokes' garrison duties continue, as detailed in a letter from Colonel C. S. Edwards:*

Oct. 4, 1861

Dear Capt

I enclose you orders for election for 2nd Lieut and Cornet[5] of your Corps. on the day you requested. I have also enclosed you Lt. Appleby's commission as your Post offices are the same and your next meeting will be time enough for him to take the oath. He is allowed 60 days from the day of election. I will visit your troop on your own parade ground this fall or winter if the Regt is not ordered out for active service. I saw Genl Tobin's notice in the paper, but did not know his company were full. I got a letter from Capt Smart about the election. I got one from him last night. His mother is extremely ill and he has countermanded his order for going into camp on the 7th inst. I intended visiting the entire Regt by companies commensing in Sept last but my parade horse died and I have not been able to get one to suit me yet. Horses are very high and no prospect of their geting any lower. I heard heavy firing of cannon in the direction of Charleston on yesterday morning between 8 and 9 o'clock. I expect to hear this evening the course of it.

Yours truly,

/s/C. S. Edwards


P.S. Rev*d* John W. Kelly is Chaplain for the Regt—I am acquainted with Mr. Crook and if there was a balancing I would give him the appointment.

| Orders | Head Quarters of the |
|---|---|
| No {illegible} | 4th Regt Cav. S.C.V. |
| | Pineville 4th Oct 1861 |


1st  An election for a 2nd Lieutenant to command in the Hammond Hussars Cavalry to fill the vacancy caused by the promotion of Lt Appleby is hereby ordered to be held at the parade ground of the troop on Saturday the 19th inst. between the hours of 11 o'clock a.m. and 3 o'clock p.m.

2nd  An election is ordered for Cornet to command in said

corps to fill the vacancy caused by the resignation of Cornet Liston at the same time and place.

Capt W. Stokes will detail the managers, hold the election, count the vote, and cause a report of the result to be forwarded immediately to the Head Quarters of the Regiment.

By order of Col Edwards

W. J. Morrall
Adj't.

*A second letter from General Tobin is received by Captain Stokes, dated October 31, 1861:*

You will perceive by the enclosed order of Col Dickens, that your company is detached for immediate service on the seacoast.

Upon receipt of this, please report to me at this place forthwith the number of your company, the kind & number of arms, etc. It is recommended that each man provides himself with a military overcoat and a piece of oil cloth to wrap up his blankets and clothes, and leather straps to strap the roll valise fashion behind the saddle and also in all cases a curb bridle. Better have a curb and a halter with leather or rope.

You[r] sword must all be ground sharp, and have a sound knot to ease the hand through of Buckskin or leather or something else.

Yours truly,

/s/ J. E. Tobin

P. S. Three other companies are attached in the same way all to come under my command on the coast.

*On November 7, 1861, Colonel Edwards writes a follow-up letter to Captain Stokes, entailing new instructions as well as news of the fighting on the coast.*

Capt

I enclose you commission for 2nd Lieut Macharry and Cornet Williams which you will oblige by handing them over to them. I have read order from Genl Tobin to put the Regt on a War footing. I have issued orders to Major Farr to hand in a report of what his Squadron is in want of. As to what the State will furnish in addition to arms, I am unable to say, but I think Canteens, Blankets (one to each man) percussion caps & cartridges. You must get your Troop in readiness to march at any time. I am expecting marching orders daily. I heard heavy fireing of Cannon in the direction of Hilton Head today. I hope Genl Ripley[6] will succeed in driving the Fleet to pieces. I heard that two vessels had been sunk this morning.

Yours very Respectfully

/s/ C. S. Edwards

*Six days later, Captain Stokes receives his orders to muster his unit and report for active service. The document is reproduced below.*

Head Quarters 4th Regt
Cav. S.C.M.
13th Nov 1861

Order No 1
Capt W. Stokes

You are hereby ordered to assemble your Troop at Walterboro on Wednesday 20th inst. fully armed and equiped for immediate actual service. You will impress Guns of any description, Horses, Mules & Wagons. For each impressment you will give a receipt for the same.

By order of Brig Genl Tobin

/s/ W. J. Morrall            /s/ C. S. Edwards

Adjt                              Col 4th Regt Cav

7

*Having complied with the call to active service, Captain Stokes describes the terrain and duties of his first assignment. All of his letters, unless otherwise indicated, were written to his wife, Eliza Jane Stokes, whom he addressed as "My Dear Wife" and signed formally as "Your Affectionate Husband, William Stokes," with his complete name. Furthermore, only those letters which convey the history of the 4th South Carolina Cavalry have been selected. Descriptions of events that pertain to family matters have, with few exceptions, been excluded.*

Camp Marrion, Bluffton
Dec 1st, 1861

You will see from the heading of this that we have moved. We arrived here yesterday evening. I am now a little over a hundred miles from home and on a very exposed point. There is a river on either side of us that the yankee fleet can pass up and the width between them is only 6 miles, so you see that unless our Picketts are very vigilant the yankees can get in our rear and cut us off from the main land. We are occupying the post of honor. I expect to go about 8 mi. down below here tomorrow with Lieut-Col Colcock to see the yankee armada. He invited me to go with him. We are under him for the present. We are quartered here in a very nice stone building. This is a very pretty village, but every house is deserted and only a few of them have the finest kind of furniture left in them. It is very destructive to see the condition of this place. I had to give up my tent when I left Pineville. We would be very well fixed if we had one more wagon and some more kettles etc.

Camp Marrion, Bluffton
Dec. 11th, 1861

We have had quite an exciting time the last two or three days, and [an] expedition went out on Spring Island on Sunday night to capture some negroes and burn the cotton on the Island. It is about 6 or 7 miles from here. 12 men volunteered from my company to go, but they only wanted 4 so 8 of the number had to remain and when they got to the levee the flat

would not carry them all and 2 had to return. Jas Williams &
George Griffis were the ones that went on. They captured 40
negroes and burned 20 bales [of] cotton. They remained on
the Island about 24 hours; the yankees had been on the Island
but none were there while the expedition stayed. Another left
this morning about 9 o'clock and has not returned yet. There
were about 200 negroes on the Island before the 40 were taken
off. They have a pack of negro dogs with them today. One
negro was killed the other day and another pretty badly shot.
The one that was killed was trying to take a gun from one of
the soldiers and he shot his brains out.

We have now 7 cavalry companies here. Capt Salley's now
arrived and the 2 Infantry Companies left here today and I am
very sorry they are gone as our duties will be more arduous and
you may be assured they are hard enough now. The men are
on duty almost every other night. I have come to the conclusion that the fighting part of war is the easiest.

Lieut McAthany did not succeed in getting off as easy as he
thought, as the Colonel commanding this post cannot receive
his resignation. William Tucker has resigned and will go home
tomorrow. The excitement to the last 2 or 3 days has prevented me for going to see the fleet yet. Chas. Hien [?] & Isaac
Liston were shot at, at Buckingham ferry the other day from
Pinckney Island, but neither of them was hit but they heard the
ball whiz by them. It was too far any how to have done them
any damage. Gen Drayton[7] is very unpopular and every one
wants him out of his command. I have not got my cooking
utencil yet, but we are doing very well now with the pots &
ovens we have gathered around here. The men and horses are
faring sumptuously now and the only thing I hate about it is
having to buy my own rations. We have good Beef, Pork,
Bacon, etc and as many Potatoes, Rutabaga, Turnips as we will
send out in the country and gather. A gentleman who has
some 15 or 20 acres of Potatoes said all of his negroes but 6
have gone to the yankees. He told me last Sunday to send my
men out and get as many as I wanted. I have two Rutabagas,
1/2 Bu. of very fine potatoes. My rice and meat I have to buy.

I have written to the Editor of the Mercury to send my paper to me here. I have seen no news since my arrival here. . . . This is the last sheet of paper I have and what little is here is sold at 5 cts for every two sheets. There were more [than] 50 of the Company would have gone in the Confederate Service, but not enough to keep the Company so I gave up all idea of getting them in. We are in the State Service and will not get more than State pay. We have sent Capt Salley to Columbia to see the Gov. to know what sort of service we are in and also to protest against the Gov. appointing Gen Tobin over our own field officers. He will return on Saturday. . . . I do not like Butler (horse) and if I can get another I will send him home yet. He is obstinate and don't want to pass strange objects.

# 1862

*Shortly after the new year, Captain Stokes and his company move yet again to continue as part of the local defense.*

Camp Hampton,<br>Jan. 15th, 1862

We arrived here safely right after dark and found all of our tents pitched or rather we are occupying tents that the Infantry had left. They are very good. The tent that I occupy is floored over with plank. We are having [a] dreadful time of it in the way of weather. It has been raining ever since we came here, off and on and I am affraid it has now set in for a steady night rain. I do not like the ground on [the] whole my tents are pitched. It is not roleing enough to run the water off, but I will move them as soon as it breaks off if I can find a more suitable place. We are furnished with almost every thing that is necessary for camp life, that is the men have cooking utencils etc, but the officers do not get any thing but plates and axe and hatchet and his horses fed.

It has been raining so that I have not been far from my tent since I have been here. I called on Peter Raysor this evening and got acquainted with his Major, who is his brother-in-law. Major Felder thinks his squadron will leave here tomorrow or next day. There will be only one other Cavalry company here then besides mine. I have only 55 men here with me, but expect we will be mustered in Confederate service tomorrow. It [is] very likely we may be here for two weeks yet.

Camp Hampton<br>Jan. 19th, 1862

We were mustered in on Friday at 12 o'clock. There was very little form about it. The line was formed and Col Preston[8] told me to have the roll called after which he told them that they were about to be mustered into Confederate Service for special service and local defence and all who had any bodily infermities or disease that would prevent them from performing the duties of a soldier to march out at the command march. He then gave the command, and to my utter surprise

13

J. S. Lynes, Wm Deas, Sam Goodwin, Jas. Kinsey, J. D. Carter & M. A. Thomas went out. The Col took their names and told me to send them to Dr. Rair in Col[umbia] for examination next day and if they got a certificate to release them. They went, but not one of them got it, and the boys have been teasing them ever since.

I went to Columbia yesterday evening and selected the cloth for uniform[s] for the company and have practically engage[d] them to be made up. It will cost $14.75 each for those who furnish the buttons.

I expect the squadron will be formed sometime next week, probably the first. We have 5 Companies here now, besides 2 Companies of the other squadron, which will leave here next Tuesday. The company Jeff Stokes is in left here to-day. We have only 2 candidates for Major of our Squadron, A. G. Salley of Orangeburg and J. P. Adams of Columbia. Of the present candidates I am desididly in favor of Adams and think he will be elected. I have abandoned the idea of running, though I believe I could have made a very good run and could possibly have been elected.

Camp Hampton
Jan. 22, 1862

We elected our Major yesterday. Jas. P. Adams of Columbia was elected. I could have been elected with all ease, if I had have come out two day[s] before the election. I was solicited by Capt O. Barber of the Chester & Fairfield Company to come out on the morning of the election, but I told him I could not consistently do it, from the manner I expressed myself to Adams, and told him furthermore that there was no chance, that it was too late, but he contended it was not and said that he would run me any how. I thanked him for his kind feelings for me, and told [him] I hope he would not run me. Nothing would stop him untill he felt round and found out it was too late and then he came to me and told me he had found out that it was too late as I had told him, that the men had committed themselves. I expect that my company will leave here in a day or two and come by home. I expect we will leave here Friday or Saturday.

Race Cruise [?],
Jan. 28th, 1862

We expect to leave here very soon, though I do not know what day. Still I think it will be the last of the week.

It was reported in town to day that 125 vessels were off New Bern, N. C. If a fight should come off, we may be sent off in a great confusion and half fixed. I am now having the Horses of my Company shod and we are getting fixed off as fast a[s] possible. I have very good tents, though they are not near as large as the officers had at Camp Hampton.

Feb. 1st, 1862

We leave here certain tomorrow, Sunday. We have been expecting to move every day for the last 4 days, which keeps us confused all the time.

*Although Captain Stokes writes of continually changing station, the mission of his company remains the same: local defense.*

Honey Hill,
Feb. 18th, 1862

The pickets get a shot at a negro occasionally, trying to make their escape to the yankees. One was shot at by a member of my Company the other night in the road on a bridge not far from here. He dropped all of his baggage and run for his life. I think he must have either been killed or hit from the way the shot cut.

I have heard very bad news from Fort Donelson this evening though I hope it is not so. I have not seen the papers, but heard it from some one that saw the papers. He said that Nashville was in the hands of the enemy and that 15,000 prisoners were taken. I tried to buy a paper but could not get one. Mr. Beech and Thos. Pinckney has just come into camp

15

and tell me that Mr. Fairey's negroes made a full attempt to get to the yankees but were stopped by the Pickets and passed themselves off as Raft hands and succeeded in making their way back.

We have two other cases of measles in camp. I rode round with the Major on Saturday last to show him my Picket and I was so sore from my ride the day before that it was all that I could do to set on the horse. (My horse is as good as ever again.) The points that I guard is very important and much depends upon our Pickets.

A battle is expected every day almost at some point on this R.R. but no one knows when.

Camp Stokes, Honey Hill
Feb. 23d, 1862

We had an alarm here on Thursday night. Capt Calhoun's Pickets came in and reported the yankees to be landing at Boyd's landing. The Major sent a Curier to me immediately to report at his Head Quarters with my command as early as possible that the yankees were landing in force. The men were just going to bed. They were soon aroused by the toot of the Horn and the ammunition that I had (which was short) was distributed, and off we put at the double quick. Everyone apparently very cold and perfectly willing to meet the enemy, which we expected to be certain to do from the report that came. When we had got about 3 1/2 miles from camp and within 1/2 mile of Calhoun's camp we met the Major, Capt Calhoun and Company. The Major and Calhoun seemed to be a little excited. The Major had sent a Lieut of Calhoun's Company to see if the report was true and he came back and reported all quiet at the Picket Station, and no enemy there. The Major then rode up to me and said he was afraid he had given me unnecessary trouble. In the meantime the Major had reported it to Col Clingman and Col Clingman sent to Coosa-whatchie and telegraphed to Gen Pemberton.[9] He got on his express train and by 4 o'clock next morning was at Col Clingman's Camp. The Gen ordered the Major to arrest

16

the fellow that started the report. I expect it will go pretty hard with him, if it is carried on. It is thought it was nothing more than a Practice. Everything is on the look out. We are expecting an attack some where on the coast every day was the reason the Gen came so quick the other night.

Camp Stokes, Honey Hill
Feb. 28th, 1862

There is some talk down here that Gen Lee will give up the R.R. and consentrate all of his forces around Charleston and Savannah though I hardly think it is so, for I do not see how we could do without the road.

Camp Stokes,
March 5th, 1862

I sent Yancey and Jones home for the remaining four men of my Company that have not yet reported: Will Lynes, J. J. Folk, P.W. Thomas & Will Thomas.

Lieut Williams and Berry sent a boy down here and he seemed to be a right smart fellow and last Saturday they give him a ticket to go and see his wife and he has not come back. It is thought he has gone to the yankees and a boat load of them got by the Pickets last Sunday night and went of[f]. Still, I do not think he had any idea of going when he went off for he left his blanket etc. He may do us a great deal of harm by telling the yankees of our precise situation, etc., though I do not consider him very intelligent.

Honey Hill,
March 7th/62

I do not think Gen Lee will hardly leave the coast, though he has moved his Head Quarters to Savannah and Gen Pemberton has command of the whole department of So. Ca., for the present. He is getting a little better since he has been promoted to a Major Gen. He has authorized leave of absence to be granted to one man from each company at a time & one Com. officer on urgent necesities, so I suppose, if an officer['s] family was ill or he, himself, leave of absence might be granted him. I feel better on the subject as he has left it in the hands of the Major. I expected to have received pay for my services before now, but have [not] received any yet. Still, I hope it will come soon.

I have a deserter, J. G. Proveaux. He will have a hard time of it when I get him again. I hear that his intention is to get to the fort. . . . Our camp was named in honor of myself, but I hardly know who gave it the name.

Camp Stokes,
March 11th, 1862

I got an order yesterday to send one recruiting officer and one private home for thirty days to try and recruit my company to 125 men. (I have 80 odd now.) So I intend to divide the time between the four officers. Lieut Appleby leaves tomorrow for seven days. I will take the last and will get 9 days, so. . . . I may get home some time the 1st of April, about the 3[rd] or 4[th] day. Still my anticipation may [be] thwarted if we have a battle before that time.

Camp Stokes,
March 16th/62

Col Clingman's Regt was ordered to New Bern, N. C. last Friday and left on Saturday. A Tennessee Regt, Col Savage came yesterday to take his place; they have a desperate name and the inhabitants of Grahamville are very sorry for the exchange, especially the ladies for several of them and his officers are said to be engaged. Capt Walker of his Regt and a Mrs. Butler got married this morning. He will leave on Tuesday next, but I heard that the Col and almost the whole Regt hated to leave. The Col is a single man and he spent a good [deal] of time around the ladies himself. Col Savage's Regt has the name of having but little respect for private property, steal everything they can get hold of, even go so far as to go in anyone's yard and kill the poultry, when there is no man.

18

I have a recruit in my company, who has been down here and knows this whole country. I took him on Friday and went out on reconnaisance expedition on Manigault Neck. Two Mr. Frippes met me there and took me all over the neck and showed me all the roads and by-paths, etc. I saw where those pickets were killed at Frippes' houses. The yankee balls cut in every direction and it is a great wonder that more of our men were not killed. I went down within sight of where we picketed when we were at Bluffton. We traveled along some very dangerous looking places, but we were very well armed. It was very profitable to me.

I have 83 men on the Roll, and expect to get 10 or 15 more during the next week. The men give me very little trouble any more and I have had but very few to punish in any way. It is very likely that we will have one or two more companies attached to our Bat[talion] and if there are we will be entitled to a Lieut Col and Major and my men want me to run for Lieut Col, though I would prefer that they would elect Adams to that office and elect me Major as I would have a light time of it. Some say they do not want to loose me as their Capt for fear they will not get such a one again. If the office is to run for I would not be at all surpris[ed] if they did not elect me Lieut Col, for they do not think so well of Adams, as he cannot do every thing they want done, and they think a great deal of me.

*General Drayton, with infantry, artillery, and cavalry, had been ordered to observe Bluffton and the roads to Hendersonville. The plan was designed to prevent the loss of the railroad bridges by moving his troops en masse to wherever the Union forces chose to attack along these routes. Captain Stokes writes of some of this activity associated with this plan.*

Camp Stokes,
March 20th/62

I have recruited my company up to 90 members and I think it will not be long before we get up to 120, as we will get a good many of those whose time will be out in April.

A portion of my company got over anxious to go in for the war [the duration] the other day and asked me to fix off a roll and let them sign with some company officers. I fixed it off an[d] you need not be surprised to hear that the whole or most of the company is in for the war. I am in now as their Capt provided enough signs the roll. We have the whole year to make it up for. If it was made up now we would have to remain in the present organization until the year went out.

p.s. 1 o'clock 21st

I have just received [an] order to go to [unintelligible] Island road and lay in wait for the enemy at or near Bluffton.

Camp Stokes,
March 21, 1862

. . . . I have now returned from what I thought this morning before day would be a big battle. I was aroused this morning by a dispatch from Gen Donelson[10] ordering me to have my company in readyness immediately to accompany the infantry and artillery. The men were arouse[d] by the sound of the horn and they [were] ordered to get their breakfast and prepare one day's rations, which was done in about 1 1/2 hours and they went on the march, to make a junction with Gen Donelson's Brigade which was soon done. He called for me and told me to take my company and go ahead of the artillery and infantry and act as an advance guard and scout the country for a mile or more ahead. . . . [M]y company was occupying an important and very dangerous position plus we made up our minds to do honor to an honorable position or die in the attempt. The Major came up with the other company after a while and the Gen turned over the command of all the cavalry to him, which I had before and he had me halted and order[ed] me to take my company still further in advance. I arrived at the point that I was ordered to some 1 1/2 or 2 hours before the remainder of the army and put out pickets on every side and remained in that position until the army came up; but just before they came up a courier came to me from where the enemy had landed and reported that they had gone back after capturing the Pickets that were at that point. That was Buckingham Ferry, where it is said one regiment landed with one Howitzer and another Regt landed at Hunting Island, the former 5 miles from Bluffton and the latter 2 miles. They have all gone back. It is reported in the Savannah [paper] that 1000 landed at Bed Bluff, but I do not place any confidence in the report as I think it all originated from the other. I feel badly to night from loosing sleep last night and have taken a little cold. I am very thankful it is no worse, for I expected to have been up all night to night and possibly one or two more, for I was under the impression this morning that we were going into a severe battle. I would not be surprised if we did not get into one soon.

I saw the grandest sight to day in the military line that I ever saw in my life before. To look down a straight and wide road for two miles or as far as the eye could see and behold a vast army of Cav, Inftry, and Artillery was grand indeed; being in the advance I had a good opportunity of seeing and the Major complimented me for the manner in which I conducted the advance guard and gave me [the] choice, either to return in the rear or take the advance again, so I chose [the] latter, for two purposes: to see the whole army and to get back earlier. I got back to camp about 2 1/2 o'clock.

Lieut Appleby could not go with us as he was too unwell and he hated it very much. The men acted nobly. I had to have some to send on Picket and had to detail that.

Camp Stokes
March 22, 1862

Capt Barber came down here with his company this evening and Capt Caughman will leave with his in the morning to take the place Barber had. The Capt & his Orderly Sergt took supper with me (Cauldwell).

I feel very well tonight again and have pretty well got over the fatigue of the big expected battle. The poor Infantry I was truly sorry for them. They were lying by the road side in every direction tired down, and some of them never got to their camps until late to day, with little or nothing to eat. My men

21

say they have seen enough of the infantry and are willing to stick to the Cavalry during the war.

We are now under the immediate command of Gen Donelson of Tenn. and his Head Quarters is remove[d] to Grahamville. The Quartermaster & Commissary Stores are moving there now, and we will have a better road to travel.

Camp Stokes,
March 23d, 1862

The report was that the yankees had landed near Bluffton and were advancing against Hardeeville or Grahamville. The Gen ordered a detachment of scouts to be sent off under a Capt and Lieut to go down & investigate the matter. Capt Calhoun & Lieut Berry with ten men from each of three companies went and returned about 3 o'clock p.m. and reports that about 800 of the enemy landing at Hunting Island 2 miles from Bluffton with 2 pieces of cannon & engaged our Pickets (from the Phillips Legion Ga.) for 2 hours, killed 2 of their horses and held Bluffton until this morning when they returned. No other damage was done on our side and we do not know the enemy loss. I had the remainder of the company in readiness all day, but all is quiet now. Still I do not know how long it will continue so. My impression is they are only making a faint here in order to attack some other place. Our forces that were at Bluffton have fallen back to New River Bridge 8 miles. I do not think that Legion can be much or they would have put it to those fellows just right, without ever troubling the rest of us.

Camp Stokes,
March 26th, 1862

All is quiet with us again but how long it will remain so I cannot say. Tonight is the night in course for another alarm. Capt Barber had a regular time of it night before last, with some negroes trying to make their escape to the yankees. The picket station at which it occured was about 1/2 mile below my camp. Three men were at the station and fired at the negroes, some 8 or 10 in number, six time[s] about 12 o'clock, and reported back to Capt B & he sent others down and they fired and one returned again and he then took all the company down, but they had all escaped by that time. He sent me word about it but, as soon as they told me that their fire was not return[ed], I concluded it was nothing much and remained in bed and slept.

I have had to stop writing to talk with Lieut Smith and O[rderly] S[ergeant] Robt Caldwell of Capt B.'s Company, who called on me to night. . . .Gen Donelson has command of this military District now and he appears to be a very kind old fellow. His Head Quarters is Grahamville. He has two daughters with him. I think he is a widower. Fort Donelson is said to be on his land. We have three Regt of Infantry near here from Ga, all new troops just organized. I hope the Tennessee Regt of Infantry near here will soon leave on account of the desperate name they have. They have but little discipline, from what I can see.

We have 92 now enrolled and all but a few now in camp. It makes a right smart show.

Camp Stokes,
March 27, 1862

There has been a good deal of shooting today in the direction of Port Royal Ferry, but I have not heard the cause. The Quartermaster and Commissary department has been moved down to Grahamville, and we have it much more convenient now and a good road. We are getting on very well now in almost every respect.

Camp Stokes,
April 21st, 1862

. . . . 5 yankees came out at one of my picket's post (Bolan's Hall) while I was home in about 1/2 mile of the post and my men motioned to them to come on, but they would not. They got in their boat after a while and went off. I think they were after plunder.

23

I could not get the money on my pay rolls in Charleston. The Quartermaster said I must get it at Hardeeville, so I went down there to day for it, but did not get it there as the Quartermaster there said he did not have the funds on hand, but would get them in a few days and write me. I got Mr. Smoke's new buggy and put two horses in it a[nd] went down in style.

I left camp at day break and got there at 8 1/2 o'clock. Gen Drayton met me at the door and appeared to be very glad to see [me] and ask[ed] me if I had ate breakfast and had my horses taken out and fed, etc. The Gen and the Quartermaster told [me] that they had received an order (in fact gave me a copy), from the Quartermaster Gen saying when the companies of the State Militia did not have Confederate members, that he must only pay four officers for every 68 men according to date of rank and the other officers must receive privates' pay. I will be sure to get my pay and I doubt whether more than 1 Lieut gets an officer's pay in my company for the Bluffton pay. . . . I have not been paid yet.

Well . . . . I suppose you have seen from the conscription act that we have to reorganize within 210 days. I think the act a very good one, and will cause us now to have a permanent army. One Major will not be re-elected and a number of men from the different companies have solicited me to run. I would not do so if I thought the Major could be elected, but the men are down on him and they say if I do not run they will bring out somebody else, so I told them I would serve them if they would elect me. I have not seen the Major since [he] has been forced out. I am very sorry that Wm. Appleby is not here, to see for himself. Still I do not think there will be any difficulty about his getting his same place, and of course the companies will all have to be reorganized before the battalion.

Camp Cuthau, Honey Hill
April 24, 1862

I have just got permission this evening to move from this place nearer Grahamville and will commence fixing off the place tomorrow and will move either on Saturday or on Sunday. The health of the camp is not very good. We have a great many

cases of Dysentery and cold, from the last sudden change. . . .
I think our camp will soon become more healthy after we move.
. . .The Major ordered me to send some men at Pirxaux and
Carter and I sent two after each and only gave them three days
to go and come in. We are being left very bare down here.
Almost all of the infantry are being moved off to Va and the
West and to Charleston. The 2 Tennessee Regt and 2 of this
State's Regt. were sent to Corinth a day or two before I left
home and Orr's Regt and Gen Gregg's[11] Brigade consisting of
3 Regt are going to Va. and the remaining two Ga Regt here
are ordered to hold themselves in readiness to go to Charleston
on a moment's notice. Then nothing will be left here but the
cavalry. The men still seemed determined to elect me over that
Major Adams. He seems to be very uneasy and is granting
almost every request the men make of him, and much more
polite than usual. The men are laughing at him about it. I tell
them that I do not intend to electioneer, that I leave it with
them. The Major thinks the old organization will be kept up
until the 12 mos. is out, but there is no grounds for it. I do
not know when the election will come off.

Camp near Grahamville
April 28th, 1862

We had a review of all the forces in this military Dist. at
Grahamville today, which would have been a grand sight if we
had had a place to maneuver in, but we had nothing but the
road. We have quite a small force here now, only 2nd Regt. Infantry, six companies cavalry & one company of Artillery. Col
Colquit of the 46th Ga Regt was reviewing officer.
　I have bought 10 head of sheep and all the wood Mrs. Garris
can spare and you must be sure to send for them next Friday or
Saturday week sure as she is to have them up for you. Wm
Garris was to get 100 lbs Sugar from his brother John for me if
he had it to spare for 10 cts a pound and was to let Phillip know
if he got it. You had better get Phillip to go out and see to it
all when you send for the sheep. I suppose N.[ew] O.[rleans]
is gone and Sugar will soon be so high that it cannot be
bought. I paid 25 cts per pound here on Saturday.

25

It is not known when we will reorganize yet. Still I do not think it will be long. I expected to be elected Major, notwithstanding the Major is granting every request that can possibly be granted. Every fellow that got a little sick now goes home on sick furlough. We have a good deal of sickness in camp. Still I am in hopes it will soon abate now, as we have men out near Grahamville. We moved last Friday evening. I am having wells dug and think I will get good water.

I sent Lieut Berry to Columbia and Lieut Williams is sick, so I am the only officer for duty. I was the only officer out with my company to day. It was Major Adams first drill and rather a mixed up affair in some things.

Camp near Grahamville
May 1st, 1862

I get my daily paper regularly and appreciate it very much. N.[ew] O.[rleans] and Fort Macon, N. C. have fallen. I almost believe that Gen Lord is a traitor. N. O. was not half defended.

I think we will reorganize about next week, though I am not certain. . . . I am well pleased with my new place.

Camp near Grahamville
May 5th, 1862

I went to Hardeeville on Saturday in a buggy [with] Lieut Williams with me to get our Bluffton money and took dysentery on the road and passed off a good deal of blood, mucous, and that night I took fever and my stomach became very irritable and I threw up constantly until about 10 o'clock yesterday. I do not know that I was ever much sicker. I had to keep [to] my bed all day yesterday and for a while could not hold my head up five minutes without vomiting. I rested tolerably well last night and feel something better this morning and hope to be up in a day or two. The officers and men gave me every attention in their power. I have no appetite at all. I got a check on the bank in Charleston for our B[luffton] money and will go to get it in a few days. I got all the officers' pay in full. The election I expect will come off on Wednesday. The Major

26

is doing his best, but he might as well quit. Our Doct[or] Tucker came on Saturday evening. I do not know how he will be liked. He seems to be a very gentlemanly fellow.

Camp near Grahamville
May 7th, 1862

I suppose W. Hiers has been telling the same tale at home that he told down here, that I would lose 20 votes in my company. I did not lose one. He asked me one morning if I believed I would lose 20 and I told him no, I would not lose one. I think he would have been against me if he could have done it slily. He was not here in time to vote. He rode up just after the election was declaired and addressed me as Major and I told him he was not here to help make me so. I entered upon the duties of the office today and issued my first order to night. By tomorrow I will be in command of this Dist., I expect, as the Ga Regt are leaving.

I bought a very fine Bay horse today for $275. and a Colonel to go on him for $35. more. I bought him from Lieut Grafton of Fairfield. You see it will take a good deal of money to prepare me for the new office. I am going to Charleston in a day or two for a uniform and Bluffton money. The Major turned over everything to me today. He seemed very much cut. J. E. Williams is my Sergeant Major and J. W. McCurry of Lancaster Quartermaster.

*Now that he has been elected, the new major shows that he is definitely enjoying the perquisites and responsibility of the command.*

Grahamville,
May 9th, 1862

It is very dusty here now. I am getting on very well in my new office and am going to drill the Bat. tomorrow evening. The following is my staff at present—J. W. McCurry Quartermaster, Lieut Foster Adj., J.E. Williams Sergeant Major. I now have command of all the forces in this Dist. and if I retain it

27

until Monday I will move my Head Quarters up to the village and occupy the office that Gen Donelson had.

The horse I bought the other day is, I think, the finest horse in the Bat. . . . He rides dilightful. . . . My horse is a dark Bay and his hair fairly shines.

Grahamville
May 13th, 1862

I moved yesterday evening. I do not think I will like it as it is more formalwise. Still I will try it a few days and will go back to the company if I do not like it.

Col W. S. Walker (who drilled us at Bluffton) is now in command of these two Dists. I am glad he has come. It will relieve me of a good deal of trouble. I am anxious to go to Charleston to get me a uniform but cannot get off yet and am afraid it will be attacked soon and I will not be able to get one.

Grahamville,
May 16th, 1862

I am quite well and have just arrived from Charleston. I went down on Wednesday. I have ordered my uniform and will have to pay $72 1/2 for it and $12 1/2 for my cap. I brought the cap with me. It is very pretty, but cost too much. I will not have money enough to pay for my uniform.

Grahamville,
May 18th, 1862

Mr. Yancey [will] take the remains of J.E. Williams home. He died last night at 1 1/2 o'clock. I do not know when I had the death of any one not related to me to affect me so much. He was a little sick when I left to go to Charleston on Wednesday and when I returned on Friday and saw him, I felt confident he could not live. Dr Tucker says he had Typhoid & dengue [?] fever combined, but my humble opinion is that he had Typhoid Pneumonia. We did all we could under the circumstances, and I hope Mrs. Williams will be consoled somewhat at knowing that friends did all they could. I have ordered an escort to accompany him for 2 miles through the village on his way. I am well; it is Sunday, but does not feel so as I cannot attend church on account of seeing Jas. off. I am getting on very well with the office and am giving entire satisfaction as far as I have heard.

Grahamville,
May 20th, 1862

I am confined to the office almost all the time except when on drill, which is every other evening. I find no difficulty in drilling the Battalion, which consist of my four companies and Beaufort Dist Troop, Capt Howard and the Charleston Light Dragoons, Capt Rutledge's. We had a very good drill this evening and I think I did credit to myself, or at least others think so.

I looked for my uniform to come this evening by express but it did not. I expect it tomorrow.

Grahamville,
May 23rd, 1862

My Adjutant and Capt McCurry went out to carouse [?] some ladies to night. The Capt is a married man but he went out with the Adj. any how. The ladies I knew are all gone off and I have not made any other female acquaintances since. I have just received my uniform this evening and it is a beautiful thing, fits to a tea all round.

. . . .Grahamville [is] on a road about 1 1/2 miles long. My Hd. Qrs. is a law office about the middle, with the tents of myself and staff just back of the office. We have five wall tents and one awning tent for the servants. All three of us that are here now have a servant a piece. We have very good water.

I am looking for Col Walker here every day to inspect the Cavalry here. I have the Charleston Light Dragoons and Capt Howard's Beaufort Dist. Troop under my command, besides the Bat. The people here are beginning to see that Adams was turned out because he was not much of an officer. I saw nothing of much interest in Charleston. It might be called

29

almost an interested camp with entirely too many officers walking about the streets smoking the best segars they can get, etc. They should be at their camps instructing their men and we would not be losing so many battles. I saw the gun boat they are building, which will not be finished in two or three months yet. They are making two and both have about the same amount of work on them.

I have not seen Col Walker yet. His Hd. Qrs. are at McPhersonville near Pocotalego.[12]

*Toward the end of the spring, the Union forces had not yet been able to land and hold any of the mainland of South Carolina. The gunboats surrounding the islands were making attacks on the batteries on shore, but were ineffectual.*

*In late May, a small force attacked at Old Pocotaligo, hoping to reach and then cut the Charleston and Savannah Railroad. Major Stokes writes of this attempt by the enemy to achieve their objective.*

Grahamville,
May 31st/62

I will give you an account of our fight at Pocotalego. Col Walker was over here with us when the enemy landed. He reviewed us and inspected us on Wednesday evening and was going back on Thursday morning on the train when he got the Telegraphic dispatch telling him of the landing of the enemy. He immediately sent orders to me to proceed immediately with the larger portion of my command in the direction of old Pocotalego. I received the orders at 1 o'clock and by 1 1/2 o'clock we were on the move for Pocotalego and were in force under some live oak that was there. I sent an advance guard on to see and report and I followed on with the main body. The place was actually in possession of the enemy at 11 or 12 o'clock, as they were trying to out flank Col Walker and he fell back to a causeway between Pocotalego and the R.R. Station (after giving them a pretty brisk fight before, when he got his horse shot through the thigh. It was only a flesh wound, and the Col told me he thought he would get over it). On the causeway he repulsed the enemy and drove them back though

advancing on the causeway. The enemy tore up the Pocotalego Bridge to cut off reinforcements from this way. Here, if
we had known it in time, they could have been easily cut off
from their gun boats. . . . We had to go 5 miles out of the way
to get round to Old Poco. and pushed on as fast as possible
after Col Walker. I came up with him at one o'clock that night.
Our Pickets and the yankees were then within 4 hundred yards
of each other, and Col Walker had stopped pursuing on account of the darkness of the night. It was then and there that
we could realize [what] war [was] and [what] battles were.
Every man that did lie down at all had to lie right by his horse
with the saddle on and his own arms on too. I laid down for an
hour or two with my sabre and all on and the skies for my cover
and slept for a little while, being very tired. At day brake we
were up and put off at the y's [yankees] again. We had 2 Regt
of Infantry, 1 company of Artillery, and about 1200 or 1500
Cav. They had pushed off just before day and got to the Port
Royal ferry and crossed over before we got there. A few were at
the ferry on the other side and the Col had a few shells thrown
over at them when they ran like good fellows. We then returned. I got back to P. Station before the cars came along and
put my horse aboard and came to Grahamville as I had transportation for myself and horse.

The yankee army from the best account I could get from a
prisoner we took the night we were so near them was 12
Infantry Companies, 3 Cavalry Co., and 1 Co. Artillery. We
killed five or six of their men and wounded nine, as well as
I could learn, and took one prisoner. And they wounded four
of our men and three are missing and I may say one of our men
were murdered by the y. Pickets the night we were so near
them. He belonged to the Rutledge Mounted Riflemen. He
was sent back by the Col to send off to carry a dispatch to be
sent off by telegraph and returning took the wrong road and
right up to the yankee pickets. They just shot a ball through,
he was so near. I saw the poor fellow lying right where he fell.
How eager the men were to avenge his death. The wounded
and those missing are from the R. Riflemen and Capt Nettles'
Cavalry Co. A Lieut is missing from Nettles.' I am sorry to

31

say that there was some bad shooting done on our side as well as that of the enemy. Our men were firing into them sometimes at not more than from 20 to 30 yds with shot guns and killed a few. Though more might have been killed than we could hear of. The first of their men that was killed was a Capt. I expect that you would like to hear something that the prisoner had to say. I asked him a great many questions as he appeared to be very full of talk. He was a foreigner who had been in the Prussian war. He was a corporal. I asked what he volunteered to come here to fight us for? He said to make something to eat. I asked him if he did not know that the Southerners were his friends? He said that the yankees did not care a cuss for them and did not care how many died. He said yes he believed, for they sent them in the worse place they could. I then asked him if there was much sickness on the Island. He said yes and if they had to stay over there all this summer, we need not go to shoot them, that they would die fast enough without. He said out [of] 103 in his Co. there were only 50 reported for duty. The others were sick. I asked him how many they had on the Island and he said 4 Regt Infantry, 3 Bat. Cav. and 1 Co. Artillery. I was really worn out when I got back about 4 o'clock yesterday. My eyes were very much inflamed, but they are better tonight. I feel totally well. I will not write . . . anymore . . . about the fight, only that this pict[ure] you saw in the papers about it had but little thought in it. Jefford's Bat. was mentioned in it and it never got there until we were 5 miles on the way coming back. The Charleston Light Dragoons was also mentioned as in it and they were under my command and with the Bat. City papers like to puff City companies.

*The war for Major Stokes remained unpredictable relative to when and, of course, exactly where. There were so many "ifs": Charleston, James Island, Savannah, or assignment out of state.*

Grahamville,
June 1st, 1862

I have no idea that Charleston will be attacked soon. It is reported today that there are 600 vessels outside of Savannah and they expect an attack tomorrow, but I somewhat doubt whether it is so. Stonewall Jackson is over in Maryland and some say he is in ten miles of Washington; that's good. Johnston and McClellan were fighting all day yesterday and McClellan was retreating and that Johnston was about to capture two Brigades if not the whole army. If it is all so, what glorious news it is for us.

We have no orders to move any where, nor do I think we will have unless we go out of the state.

Grahamville,
June 6/62

I suffer a good deal with my mouth and throat. Still I am up all the time and attend to all the duties of the office, but cannot drill the Battalion, which I regret very much as I was beginning some new drills that are of great importance to the Battalion if we should get into battle.

I received an order from Gen Pendleton calling back immediate[ly] all officers & those who are absent from camp and therefore none will be allowed to return [home]. We are also ordered to be ready to enter into action immediately, which I consider equivalent to march orders. It is owing to the attack on Charleston and it is thought that the enemy will make another attack upon this R.R. in order to cut off communications between Charleston and Savannah to keep either of those places from sending reinforcements when they make a full attack against them. I am a little uneasy about Charleston and our force is so small there, that I am afraid they may take the city with overwhelming forces. Still you know I am always hopeful. If Charleston should be taken, I am of the opinion that we will be moved from here but where to I do not know.

Grahamville,
June 12th, 1862

I was not officially engaged, but had company until
11 o'clock. Dr. Pleasant, the Post Surgeon and a very pleasant
man, comes round frequently and sits with me until that hour.
He used to be the U. S. Consul to Mexico and with all a very
interesting man.

The news from Charleston was not so good on yesterday and
I am in hopes they will fight it out at once. I have been told
that the city is to be defended street-by-street and that they
are building casemate[13] batteries in the burnt District. If that
is the case it will never be taken. As soon as they do what they
are going to do I think I can get off to go home. I am so anxious to see you all and how things look around home.

Grahamville,
June 18th, 1862

It seems from what I can hear that the yankees really intended an attack on us the other night and was thwarted by the
pickets being on the alert. There were eight flats[14] seen to leave
the opposite side of the river the next morning after the dense
fog that was there. When I left the river had cleared off.
I expect to wake them up on the other side some of these
nights if they are not on a sharp lookout to pay them for it.

Three of Capt Appleby's men (Sergt J. J. Carter, Corp Saml
Goodwin and Chas Harrison) will be tried in a day or two for
trying to fight and drawing guns on each other. I would not be
surprised if it did not go pretty hard with them. They are now
under arrest.

Grahamville,
June 19th, 1862

I went down to Palmato Point on Hogs neck[15] a day or two
ago and with a spy glass could see about 20 miles below three
vessels and a gun boat very distinctly.

Dr D. Tucker has been removed from here and Dr A. W.
Burnett came today. He is a young man and has a very good

countenance, but I do not know how he will take. . . . Dr Pleasant is the Post Surgeon and has charge of the hospital. He comes round to see me every day and appears to think a great deal of me. He is from Va and of a high family.

Grahamville,<br>
June 22nd, 1862

. . . . I was out on an expedition last night and got only 1 1/2 or 2 hours sleep, though I slept some since I returned. I took a detachment of 12 men from each company and went over on Lemon Island where the yankees were reported as being on frequently. I started with four boats to take them over with but on the way the largest and best boat is broke down, about a mile from the place of embarcation and the others would only take over about 15 men at a time. Therefore I concluded to take over only two turns 30 men and left the other 30 on this side of the river. The boats had to be rowed about 3 or 4 hundred yards before it could land. We moved at the double quick for the only dwelling there was on the Island and scowed [scoured ?] the woods as we went. We found at the house 3 old negroes and a child left by their masters as they would have been an expense to him and worth nothing. We also found 250 or 300 Bu[shels] of corn and about enough Sea Island cotton in the seed to make 3 or 4 Bales of Ginned Cotton. The yankees had been over there and had the negroes putting the cotton up in the seed in bags of from 150 to 200 lbs. each, which I suppose they call Bales. I was very anxious to get the corn off for our own use, but it would have been [necessary] to have carried [it] at least 1/2 or 3/4 of a mile in the least, and the negroes said that a large force, some 60 or 100 had left there the day before, and while we were over on the Island two signal guns fired and some of the party said they saw a gun boat down the river so the torch was applied to the corn and cotton and fodder and we left for the main land again, thinking we had done a good night's work. The property that was destroyed was worth at least $800, all of which was completely in the hands of the enemy. It was a pretty bold adventure, but we must be doing something.

35

*Major Stokes had been anticipating obtaining a leave to visit his family and to take care of personal business concerning his farm. The recent duties had prevented his applying for it until now. Before being able to write the request, a new responsibility presented itself.*

Grahamville,
June 25th, 1862

I received an important order from Col Walker, which required my personal and immediate attention and which it may take me some time yet to execute fully. Thinking that he might think very strange of my application [for a leave] under the circumstances, I concluded I had better not apply yet.

*There is no mention of exactly what the "important order" was, but a few days later, Major Stokes received a written order from higher headquarters, reproduced below.*

Hd Qrs 3*rd* Mil Dist
McPhersonville
June 28, 1862

Maj W*m* Stokes
Major

I am instructed by the Col Comdg to say in reply to your communication of the 27*th* inst. that as Martial law has never been proclaimed over this Military District, the only disposition to be made of the matter to which his attention has been called will be to turn the parties charged with the selling of spiritous liquors, if sold without a lisence, over to the civil Authorities to be dealt with as the law directs.

The liquor taken from said parties, if fit for the use of the sick in the Hospital can be placed in the hands of the Asst Surgeon; if not it should be destroyed.

Very Respectfully,

/s/A G Hally
AA

Grahamville
June 29th, 1862

I have had about 65 gal. of Whisky seized and taken from a fellow here who was selling it to the soldiers here. Some that one of Capt Barber's men bought and got drunk on liked to [have] kill[ed] him. The majority of the citizens are assisting me, succeeding in finding out the Liquor, though there are a few rascals who are trying to cloak for the guilty party. I think I have all now that the party had. A lady put me in the way of getting 60 gal of it.

I am going to McPhersonville tomorrow to see Col Walker and will see how long before he thinks I can get to home.[16]

We have heard of the glorious victory at Richmond. I heard this morning by a passenger on the train that a telegraphic dispatch came to Hardeeville to Gen Drayton that our army captured 40,000 prisoners and 3 Gens—good if true. Also that the only chance to Gen McClellan's to escape was by his Balloon.

Grahamville,
July 10th, 1862

I arrived here safely on yesterday at 10 o'clock. I did not come all the way on the day I left, as I concluded it was too hard on my horses. I stayed at Capt Guest's and left there at 4 o'clock A. M. I am very tired tonight, having not long returned from a march of 20 miles. Col Walker sent a dispatch to me at one o'clock, that he expected a battle and to come to his assistance with all the force I could spare. Rapidly I gathered them and started and moved as rapidly as the heat would permit me and when I got nearly to Coosawhatchie a courier from the Col met me with a dispatch saying that the demonstration of the enemy were of such a nature as not to need my cavalry and that I could return to Grahamville. The men were very disappointed, for they were in high anticipation at the thought of getting into a battle. The enemy came up with two gun boats to Port Royal Ferry and were shelling the woods and it is said they landed four boat loads. Infantry was sent up from

Hardeeville and the train is now (9 o'clock) passing the depot taking them back, so I think the affair must be at an end for this time.  It was on account of an anticipated attack on this road that I was ordered back, from what I can learn.  The yankees say (I have heard) that they mean to take this road by all means, that we can concentrate troops too easily with it.

Everyone seemed very glad to see me back, both soldiers and citizens.  I feel very much refreshed this morning after a good night's sleep and hope I will not have to go to a false alarm again though I do not suppose that was a false alarm yesterday. I do not know the particulars of it but suppose from all the information I have that the gun boats came up and shelled the woods around for a while.

I think it very probable that we are like[ly] to have [a] pretty warm time down here, as I think the enemy want to get on the main land somewhere and this is the most accessible to their gun boats.

[There is an] order in yesterday's paper of the Adj & Inspt Gen S. Cooper, relative to the men over 35 years and those under 18 years of age.  He says they will have to serve their twelve months out and some to stay over.  So I expect all those who had been discharged will be ordered back.  Shudder.  Wm B. Risher and others will hate it very much.  I hate it for them if they have to come back and I see no other chance than for them to have to return.

*Colonel Walker sends a letter to Major Stokes with instructions pertaining to the grave situation brought about by the Union forces' sporadic raids.  It is reproduced below.*

Hd. Qtr. McPhersonville
3d Dist.
July 12th

Maj. Wm Stokes.
Maj:
I advise you to have placed in readiness at some secret point convenient to Boyd's Landing a large row boat with the oars, and a canoe that will hold three men.

Have it done at the earliest practicable moment, as they will be required for immediate use, perhaps tonight.

Also send some one with a glass to reconnoitre whether any one of the enemy can be seen on Port Royal Island

Very respectfully

/s/W. S. Walker
Col. Cmdg.

*The next day, a second letter from Colonel Walker gives additional instructions, modifying the orders of the previous day.*

Hd. Qrs. McPhersonville
July 13th

Maj: Wm. Stokes
Major:
Upon information obtained yesterday in regards [to] the enemy, I expected to have used the boat and canoe last night. In the afternoon, however, matters had changed, which prevented the immediate use. They may be required however soon.

Very respectfully,
Yr. obdt. servt.

W. S. Walker, Col. Cmdg.

Grahamville.
July 13th, 1862

A soldier's life is one of sudden changes, and I try to meet them as easy as possible. I am very well and have got every thing to going on smoothly again. I received an order yesterday from Col Walker, saying that those men who were discharged under the conscription act, was discharged under a wrong construction of the act. Therefore the discharge was illegal and they must be ordered back to their companies, so I have ordered the Capt of the companies to order them back.

There are more [Yankees] now than there were some time

ago. The two gun boats that shelled at Port Royal Ferry the other day came by two of my most important Picket Posts and stopped out in the river for some time and looked all around with their spy glass and then went on down. They may intend making their next demonstration in this direction.

I have no idea that I will move from here soon unless run off by the enemy. I have just heard, though not officially, that this post is to be strengthened by sending some Infantry and Artillery here.

Grahamville,<br>July 17th, 1862

We are having an accession to our force here. Maj. Abney's Bat. sharp shooters are to be here tomorrow. The Major got here last night, with no camp equipage at all and he is staying here with me. One of his Lieut came on this evening. His men will be here tomorrow. I outrank the Major and will therefore still be in command of the Post. I had enough to do before and will now have my duties almost doubled. The Major is from Edgefield Dist and a very pleasant man. When we get all of his Bat. here, which is 3 Companies, I think we can stand the yankees a good fight. I also expect two pieces of artillery here soon.

*In his comments of July 13, concerning the activity of the Union gun boats, Major Stokes felt it inevitable that other landings would eventually take place. Colonel Walker sends another communication relative to this kind of action.*

Hd Qrs. 3d Mil. Dist.<br>McPhersonville, S. C.<br>July 20th

Maj. Wm. Stokes
Cmdg. 2d Battal. Cavl.
Maj:

Capt. Stephen Elliott will go to Grahamville tomorrow morning for the purpose of making a boat expedition against the enemy's pickets. He will take a four pounder to be placed

40

in one of the boat. He took men enough with him to man one boat. I desire you to furnish men enough to man another to accompany him. Two boats will be allowed to accompany him if you find it expedient. The whole force to be under his command.

Very respectl.<br>Yr. obdt. sevt.

/s/W. S. Walker<br>Col. Cmdg.

P.S. I would call your attention to some extracts from attached letter from Hilton Head as very probably indicating the plans of the enemy in operations along the coast in Mercury[17] of 17th inst. W.S.W.

July 21st/62<br>Grahamville

Capt Elliott came down this evening with some of his artillery to make an expedition to Bufort[18] Island to capture some y-pickets. I furnished him two Lieuts and 30 men. There are some flying reports that my Batt. will be ordered to Hardeeville or Bluffton but I do not know what grounds there is for it and hope it is not so, as it seems we are only to supply the place of Lt Col. Colcock['s] Batt. which is now down there to allow them to come here. I think it would be very unjust and wrong in any *Commander* to remove a number of troops from a locale that they knew and had been so long defending, to another, in which they would likely to be more sickly.

*The reports are true, and Major Stokes writes that his change of station is politically rather than militarily oriented.*

Grahamville,<br>July 23d/62

I am ordered to take my Batt. down in the neighborhood of Bluffton to change with Lt Col Colcock. I think it an imposition on us, to gratify Lt Col Colcock's wishes. The plea for it is

41

for Lt Col Colcock to get his Batt together, and by coming here he only gets one more company with him and I think it would have been much better to have moved one Co. than four. I expect to leave here on Friday and will arrive here [there?] on Friday night. I will go up and see Col Walker to day and try to get him to postpone my going for a week longer in order that the men may get paid off. He (Col Walker) says that the order eminated from Gen Pemberton at the solicitation of Lt Col Colcock. I do not think there is any chance to get it changed, but I am in hopes it will be prolonged. The men hate it very much. . . . I had much rather that my orders had been to go to Va or Chattanooga, not that I am particularly anxious to go there but I cannot bear the idea of being made a fool of. I thought Lt Col Colcock was above as low a trick as he has been guilty of.

Capt Elliott did not accomplish any thing on his expedition.

Grahamville,
July 24th/62

I will leave here tomorrow morning for my new station. I went to see Col Walker to get the time postponed but he would not consent. He says the order came from Genl Pemberton, but I am beginning to think that he had as much hand in it as Genl Pemberton, for I am sure he could have prevented it if he had tried. He knew that I had been served a mean trick and could not look at me right about it. He would keep talking about it and making all sorts of apologies and every one that he made I met him on with something to refute it. I finally got him so bad off for an apology that his answer was that it was wise to change troops to different stations occasion- ally. Now when they have remained here a while I will go to him and use the same argument on him again.

Camp Jackson
May River,
July 27th, 1862

This country is completely deserted, only one old man living here. This camp is about 2 miles above Bluffton. The bank on which my tents are pitched is about 30 or 40 ft. above high water and one of the prettiest places you ever saw. The water here is very salt[y] and here is the place to boil it. My tent is in 20 ft. of the bluff.

There is an old man, Mr. Crowell, who lost 60 negroes; in fact, all but three old negroes and with them and one large kettle and a pot, he makes a 1/2 bushel of salt each day, and boils only in the day. Mr. Crowell is very kind to me and sends me butter milk every day and last night a fine curd. Since I started [writing] I stopped to ride down to Bluffton. It looks like desolation and the once beautiful village is now grown up with weeds.

The sand flies are very bad here when the wind is from the inland. Last night they troubled me a great deal, but the night before they did not trouble me at all. I expect to move to New River soon if I can find a good camping place. I may move my camp in a few days as it is too much exposed to the enemy's gun boats here. Still, I will not be far from here then, and all that I would like to move for is to get my baggage and tents farther from the river.

Camp Jackson,
July 30th, 1862

He [Colonel Walker] and Col Ellis came down here this morning and will remain here with me until tomorrow morning. They think my camp perfectly delightful on account of the fine breeze here all the time. We are having fish almost every meal. This is the greatest river for fish I ever saw. It seems to be alive with fish. I'm better satisfied with my place, though the yankees are trying to capture my pickets. Last night they surrounded my two pickets at Bear's Island and they got into a creek with their horses and dodged them, so they say. They say that the y— were about 15 in number. My duties are so large that I cannot send more than two to a post. I only wish they may follow it up and I will show them how it is.

Camp Jackson,
July 31st, 1862

I succeeded in getting a five days leave of absence from Col Walker this morning to go to Charleston to try and procure some ammo for my command and also to see about the pay of the troop who have not been paid off in five months. I will leave here on Saturday morning, and as I cannot attend to any business on Sunday, I will run up to Branchville on Saturday night, if nothing turns up between now and then.

I have been riding all day since Col Walker left (which was about 8 o'clock) to the different pickets' posts and am tired enough to night. I shot at my first yankee today across a river about 5 or 600 yds across the river at Buckingham Ferry with a long range rifle that is gaged for 1700 yds. The first crack I took they ran like good fellows, or in other words they "skedaddled." I took two other cracks at different times and they did likewise. The fire was not returned until after we left.

Camp Jackson,
August 7th, 1862

I arrived here safely last night about dark and had not been here more than half an hour when two of my pickets (from Capt J. C. Calhoun's Co.) brought in three full-blooded yankees to my quarters, who came a little too near their post at Bear's Island, fishing, thinking there were no pickets at that point. My pickets saw them for some time and secreted themselves until they got within about 75 yds when they drew their guns on them and ordered them to come to shore, which order they obeyed immediately. The prisoners were fine looking fellows, from N.[ew] H.[ampshire], the 3d Regt. and were in the James Island fight. They say they never saw bullets fly as they did from our men in their lives and never want to see them again. Two of them were very talkative, but the other had nothing to say and seemed to be in a deep study all the time. They wanted the war to end, but still thought they would whip us. I sent them to Col Walker this morning and he sent me word to keep fishing. Lieut Berry who took them up says he was the best pleased in the world. The fellows were well dressed.

Camp Jackson,
August 9th, 1862

Capt Mickle went out last night on another expedition and the yankees are shelling furiously in the direction that he went. I have heard over fifty guns and they are still firing. I suppose it is some 6 or 7 miles from here in a direct line. It is now 12 o'clock M.[idnight] and I hardly think they intend making a landing. If they do the pickets will report it directly. Those prisoners we took the other day said they were reinforced down there, but I do not believe it. They were tired enough of the war and one said if he was exchanged and sent back down here again, that he would have to come over and be taken again, that he never wanted to get into a battle again. They said that the negro Brigade over there numbered about 5 or 600 and were armed with spades, etc., but was promised guns soon, that they were the damnedest fools they ever saw, and that you could not learn them any thing, that they did not care how many of them we killed; that this was caused by men about them, and the men that caused it were out of the war, that is, they mean the prominent abolishionists keep out.

I expect to get my pay again in 3 or 4 weeks, and expect to keep all of that on hand except enough to pay Capt Jones $235 for the horse I bought from him (Beaureguard).

The men have been paid off today for 2 mos. and I expect they will get the other two months pay and bounty[19] in a week or two.

Camp Jackson,
August 14th, 1862

I have just got through with my dinner, and a rather poor one it was too. Fried middling bacon, rice and clabber. I have had nothing like vegetables since we came down here. Still I suppose we should be thankful [in] these war times that we have any thing at all to eat. We get very fine fresh beef twice a week & I enjoy our fine breeze here now very much these hot days.

We have very little sickness in camp. You heard wrong. Still I am afraid we will have it yet.

Beaureguard (my grey horse) is either foundered badly or has a disease that a great many of the horses here are dying up with. He seems to have very little use of his limbs at all, can hardly stand on them. I am afraid he will never be any use to me again. I drove him to Hardeeville on day before yesterday and yesterday. Capt McCurry and Yancey drove him there again and this morning he was in that fix. Capt McCurry went on up the country to fix his bond as Quartermaster and Yancey drove the horses back.

Camp Jackson
August 20th, 1862

I am very much troubled tonight with different things. A few furloughs are being granted again and I am being troubled a good deal with them. There is an expedition gone out of 150 men under Capt Elliott on Pinckney Island and that is giving me some trouble, though none of my men are on this expedition.

Capt McCurry's appointment [as Quartermaster] has been approved by the War department and he has gone to execute his bond.

Camp Jackson,
August 22nd, 1862

Mr. Smoke and Thomas have made some 8 or 10 bushels of salt and expect to leave in the morning for home. I will send

46

this by Mr. Thomas. It will get to you before the next mail. Some of the salt they made is very pretty, and it all could have been so if they had taken proper care with it. I am anxious for you to get through pulling fodder and send me down some hands to boil salt. Have you received the salt I sent? Tell Doct that I want four hands and some four or five kettles and one two-horse and one four-horse wagon and two of the hands must bring axes. He will want some buckets, dippers etc., also a piece of coarse cloth to tie over the barrel to drain the brine from the salt.

The expedition I wrote you about that went off under Capt Elliott of the Beaufort Artillery was pretty successful. He went over to Pinckney Island with 150 men and surprised a company of yankees of 60 men and captured 36 prisoners and killed and left wounded some 12 or 15 others. None of our men were killed but 8 were wounded, three of which I am afraid will die and the worst of it is that our men were wounded by some of our own men that went over. Which was owing to some of the men not obeying orders and getting mixed up among the enemy. Some of our men were too brave and broke ranks and run helter skelter ahead of the others and when a yankee would break through between them the men that were behind would fire on the y— and hit as many of our men as they drove off the y's. All of our men are slightly wounded but three. They [Yankees] all belong to the same company that those did that my pickets took some time ago. The most of them were good looking fellows and they say they are heartily sick of the war and if they can only get home again they will not come down here anymore. They say that more troops have been coming in on Hilton Head. I suppose the Savannah dam [?] is drawing them back, if it be true that any have come. Two small gun boats came round yesterday and shelled several of my picket posts and the woods in general but without doing any damage. One shell, a 32 pounder, fell in a few feet of Lieuts Bell and Settle, which if it had exploded would have killed them both, I expect.

The evening before Capt Elliott went over to Pinckney Island, Lieuts Berry & Williams & myself were at the picket post he was to start from (Bear's Island) and I called on him

47

and told him I would be glad to give him any assistance that I could. He thanked me and said he would be glad if I would send him a canoe. When I returned yesterday a report was circulated in camp that I was offered the Command of the expedition and would not take it. I gave it the lie and proved it so and told all the Capts to call up their men and make strict inquiries for the author and Capt Appleby reported to me that two of his men were willing to swear that the first they heard of it was the evening that I went down to see Capt Elliott, and that they heard Yancey say so. What was his motive for telling such a tale I cannot say or think. I brought him up and gave him a lecture on it. He says he does not remember any thing of it. He is heartily sick of the deed if he does the like again. I will put him back in the company.

*As it became necessary to increase the number of units and men under arms, new regiments would be created. Interspersed throughout the correspondence for the next several weeks are letters concerning the formation of one of the new regiments of cavalry.*

Camp Pritchard,
August 31, 1862
Beaufort District, S. C.

I hear that our Battalion, Morgan's Battalion, the Charleston Light Dragoons and another company are to be consolidated into a regiment and that Capt. Rutledge, of the C. L. D., is to be appointed Colonel, myself Lieut. Colonel and Major Morgan, the Major. The regiment is to be the 3rd Regiment of Cavalry.[20]

General Pemberton told me the other day that all the Cavalry was to be organized into regiments.

*There is no correspondence for most of September and parts of October because Major Stokes was on a medical furlough for thirty days due to a hemorrhage of the lungs.* [See Appendix I, No. 4.]

Camp Prichard[21]
Sept 25th 1862

I am again at my post where I arrived today about 12
o'clock. I did not get to Hardeeville until this morning about
3 o'clock as the train ran into 4 cows two miles this side of
Pocotaligo, which threw the engine and tender off the track and
we did not get off from there until 1 1/2 o'clock this morning.
It was in a cut and no one got hurt, but the engineer, who was
only slightly hurt.

*A letter from a certain G. M. Yancey informs Major Stokes that
the Regiment of Cavalry about to be formed will have as its commander Captain Rutledge, whom the men do not want.*

H'd 2nd Batt Cav S.C.V.
Camp Pritchard
Oct 8th 1862

Maj. W. Stokes,
Sir,
I received your letter to night and I am instructed and
requested by Capt Barber, Capt McCurry, the Adjutant, and a
host of others to answer it immediately and tell you to oppose
being thrown into a Regiment. If you will oppose it they say
our Batt will not be thrown into a Regt. Capt Rutledge knew
that it would require your consent; had he not been aware of
that, he would not have visited you on the subject. The whole
command is indignant at it. Some of the captains, being of the
opinion that you could prevent Capt Rutledge's attempt, will
think hard of you if you don't try. Capt Barber says "surely
the major will not sell us all to Rutledge in that way, when he
could prevent it simply by a protest." They are all anxious
to know whether you agreed to it or not. They think if you
objected it will not be formed into a Regt. That other major
ranks you I expect.
I am trying to get Jim's dues. Capt McCurry refuses to pay
it. You will please certify, as major, to what Capt Appleby does
as captain. I see by an order and, also, by army Regulations

49

that a Battalion is allowed a Sergeant Major. I learned it since you left. So it will be necessary for you to certify to what you know about Jim's death and dues.[22] You can take your information from what Capt Appleby certifies to. My mother-in-law will see you on the subject.

There was not a shot from our Batt against the yankees the other day. The enemy only fired or throwed shells. I gave you nearly all I knew about it in my last [letter]. I, not having a horse and Capt Barber wanting me to stay at H'd Qrs as Capt McCurry was absent, did not go down with the Batt. The main body of the command did not go very close to the yankees. Some few men were in two or three hundred y'ds of them. We have orders from Walker to Patroll the whole country and have the pickets visited night and day by coms'd officers. He suspects spies at being over here. So do I.

Please let my wife know when you will return. As usual we are without butter and potatoes. I brought a good lot when I came, but they are gone. Don't [think] that I am hurting. All I want is that you will bring some butter and potoes and grists from some place, as we can not get them here, not even for the money.

I am truly sorry to hear to night that we are defeated at Corrinth.[23]

Your very respectful servant

/s/G. M. Yancey

P. S. Capt McCurry received a letter from the Secretary of War stating that this is the 10th Batt Cav S.C.V. Please answer immediately, mentioning the facts as to letter letting us know what steps you intend taking in regard to Capt Rutledge and the Regt.

G. M. Yancey

*On the following day, another letter opposing the appointment of Captain Rutledge as commanding officer of the future regiment is addressed to Major Stokes.*

Camp Pritchard
Oct. 9th 1862

Maj. Wm Stokes
Maj:

To my surprise and regret I read your letter to the Regt's Major stating that Capt Rutledge still persists or rather strives for the colonelcy of the Regt to be formed of yours, another Batt and companies. It is astonishing to see what measures have been taken on the part of others not to your knowledge and on being questioned give in black and white their ignorance of such a thing other than rumored at that. They have such and will not take any step toward it as they regard a commission hunted down by political influence as not worth a farthing. The entire command is opposed to being formed into a Regt unless you are the commandant of the same. As far as myself I can do and say nothing more than I have expressed my desire and remain under your command either as an independent corps or Regt if you wish. Should Rutledge be appointed Col it will throw me out of my position which will force me to enter the Regular Army, but would not have you think that my own commission and position prompts me to write the way in which I have. 'Tis throu respect and esteem. And I am assured that I represent the entire command in my letter. By & with the advice and consent of Capt Barker I wrote to Richmond sometime past in good measure for my commission which I am daily expecting.

I am directed by Capt Barker to say that you oppose entry into any organization without you are promoted to colonelcy. And that you also never expressed to Capt Rutledge and the War Department your objection to being formed into a Regt on terms other than those above stated and think you will be sustained in it as Lt Col by A. A. Evans from Richmond has expressed his appreciation of similar class of Batt's of Cav most effective and beneficial to the service.

With the assurance of
high esteem
I remain your O.S.

/s/J. R. Massey

P. S.  Capt Barker said with [unintelligible] to Richmond writing a protest—& if a Regt must be formed apply for Colonelcy.  Lt Col Ly said independent Corps with Batts are more preferable and Regt are not formed only when parties concerned prefer and insist on it.  The "Log" is now on a tour of inspection of this department.  By reason for stating that—I would be thrown out of position, were afraid that you would *think* I were working for *myself*, not caring or assisting your welfare at all only for self appraisement.

*The behind-the-scene activity concerning resistance to the formation of the new regiment continued apace. Captain Rutledge, himself, writes what appears to be the final, "quasi-official" word on the subject.*

Oct. 16, 1862
McPhersonville
Camp Ch[arleston]
Lgt Hussars

Major William Stokes
Dear Major

I received your letter of the 12th last night while on picket, and answered it at the first moment.  I am not surprised at the wish of the Battalion to retain their separate organization.  Such is the wish of my own company.

I do not believe my wish would ever induce them to enter into any larger organization.  Nothing but the conviction that it has to come and the desire to be as agreeably situated as possible under the new state of things, has led them to assent to it. As without necessity Col Walker here told me that Battalions would not be thrown together without their consent.

I sent Lieut-Col Ward [?] at Charleston to day before their Gen'l. the correspondence of Major Emmanuel and Capt Pritchart as well as yours, and today I read your letter more times. He has also. I received a letter of 14 Oct from that officer today in which he says "I have seen Col Gonzales and he took yours today of 14 inst. and went into it with Gen'l Beauregard and showed him the letter. He says the Gen'l assessed it first with your prognosis was that he would wait no longer for Major Emmanuel's detachment. [The] Gen'l will be able to judge from these facts what he means. I expect all the better with comments or *not*. If you have doubts upon the subject—don't. You can keep out if, such as arguing about you have better go to the city and see the Gen yourself. If so take this letter with you, and let him see and you will find the facts—easily as I have stated to you—Unless the General has changed his opinion *entirely* within 48 hours, your Battalion will be *obliged* to enter into some regiment or *other*—I regret the necessity which compelled you to write to me the letter of the 12th—It may lead the General to make some changes in the organization, and I would be very sorry for it—as I think a union of the Command contemplated would be more agreeable than any other[24]—I feel myself bound however to send your letter immediately to Gen Beauregard, and then he will as you say do as he sees fit—

Yours very Respectfully.

/s/ B H Rutledge
*Capt, Ch Lgt Hussars*

*Despite evidence to the contrary, Major Stokes changes his mind after receiving Captain Rutledge's letter. Perhaps the political influence that Rutledge possessed convinced Stokes not to offer further resistance to his battalion's being incorporated into a regiment that would be commanded by an officer junior to himself.*

Camp Pritchard
Oct 16, 1862

I arrived here safely tonight and am feeling pretty well.
The y—s gun boats came up my River last Monday again and
destroyed Mr. Lawton's salt works about a mile above Mr.
Cowell's, the boats going up to there. Some five men acting as
the advance guard of the Batt. secreted themselves on the bank
and when one of the boats got in about 2 or 300 yds. of them,
the deck being covered with the y— the five fired upon them,
one of them firing at the fellow in the masts and they say he
came down at the double quick. They think they killed some of
them. Of course they had to leave in a hurry as the boat commenced throwing shells and grape.

Camp Pritchard,
Oct. 19, 1862

I did not find the Battalion half as much opposed to going
into a regiment as they wrote me. All are pretty well in the
notion of going in.

*An attack was launched against Old Pocotaligo on October 22 by
Union forces under the command of Brigadier General John
Milton Brannan, who had sailed from Hilton Head on the evening
of October 21. The objective was to destroy the railroad and the
bridges on the Charleston and Savannah line. General Brannan
split his forces; one was to march up the road to Old Pocotaligo, while
the other was sent by boat up the Broad and then along the
Coosawhatchie.*

Hardeeville
Oct. 23d, 1862

Communication was cut off yesterday and no train came
through. We beat them [Yankees] back five to one. We lost
about 60 killed and wounded and the Y— about 2 or 300
hundred.

I rested pretty well last night and did not cough so much.
Still I cough a good deal yet. I am boarding here to see if I

54

cannot get clear of this cough in a few days, three or four and if I cannot I expect to come home again & I expect to stay until I get entirely well or resign.

The fight at Coosawhatchie I cannot give you the particulars. You will doubtless get them from the papers today. We could hear cannonading distinctly all day and about night the roar was incessant. The enemy got possession of the R.R. at Coosawhatchie, but had time to only tear up three or four bars of iron and cut down the telegraph pole and fire into the train that had the 17th Regt in it (Ellis'), killing Maj Harrison and the fireman and wounding a few others when they were repulsed from there. Another column advanced on Pocotaligo at the same time, but our force there being more, they were kept in check until night when they all returned to their boats. After the enemy got possession of the road, it was reported in my camp that they were advancing against Robertville 20,000 strong, which if it had been so, would have completely surrounded us down and several of the officers wanted me to fall back, but I told them that I could not do it, until I got positive information that it was so. Then I should try to cut my way through with the Batt. I had every thing packed up for a move and kept out a strong picket. It is time we have rather a critical situation, New River being in our rear and the bridge subject to being bound up by a small force coming up the river, which can be easily done. Still, I prefer being taken than to act cowardly. Col Walker paid me and the command a high compliment about our action and management with the gun boats the other day and sent the report I made to him of it to Gen Beauregard. I saw Gen B in Charleston but did not get an interview with him. He is a small man, hardly as tall as Shidre [?], but with a large chest. I cannot tell you anything more about the Regt.[25] I wrote to Gen B– on the subject but have no answer yet.

*The battle of Pocotaligo and the successful defense of the Coosawhatchie Bridge brought to a close the aggressive actions of the Union forces to establish themselves on the mainland of the coast of South Carolina for the year 1862. Furthermore, there is no extant correspondence until late in November.*

Mill's House, Charleston, S.C.
Nov. 24th, 1862

I met up [with] my friend Capt Courtenay to night, who addressed me as Lt Colonel, and said he had been confidentially informed that Capt R. had been made Colonel and I promoted to Lt Colonel and that the order would be extended in a day or two and wanted me to put another star on my collar[26] before I left the city. I told him I would wait for the order.

I saw Col Daring of Genl Gist's[27] Staff, a few minutes ago and he told me that he had heard it too, so it must be true.

Camp Pritchard,
Nov. 27th, 1862

I arrived safely in camp on Tuesday evening and found my staff comfortably situated in Dr. Pritchard's house, where I wrote them to move. I am almost as comfortably situated as if I was at home as far as quarters are concerned. There is a great deal of furniture in the house [and it] is the greatest objection I have to it, though Dr P– has given us the use of all of it we wish. Our staples are rather light. The commissary does not issue any flour, lard or bacon to the men and will not sell any to the officers. Consequently we have no flour, lard or bacon and cannot buy it. Still we get on pretty well with Beefs and tallow. We have a little butter just now, but will soon be out.

I have had to arrest one of Barber's Lt's. and some of his privates and some of Capt A– privates since my return for horse racing.

Camp Pritchard,
Dec 4th, 1862

The Abolitionists fire a few big guns occassionally. I know nothing of the taking of Savannah, nor did I think anyone entertained such an idea.

Camp Pritchard,
Dec 7th, 1862

It is very cold and I have to get up before day in the morning to meet the cars[28] at Hardeeville to go to Pocotaligo to see Genl Walker, also to get some ordnance stores.

I hear that Small Pox is in Savannah and I have stopped letting the men go over there, though I thought of going over myself this week to buy some flour for the mess.

My uniform[29] is admired by almost everyone that sees it. I expect to wear it to Pocotaligo tomorrow. My pants are rather tight at the waist and I expect to send them back and have a piece put in behind. The coat is also rather small around the waist.

Camp Pritchard,
Dec. 8th, 1862

I have not heard anything more definite about the Regt. It seems to be a general talk that it will be formed very soon. What causes the delay I know not. I expect to go up to see Genl Walker next week & will possibly hear [about the regiment].

Camp Pritchard,
Dec. 9th, 1862

I think my health has improved a good deal since my return to camp. I have not spit up any blood for some time, though my nose is still sore, which is very disagreeable.

Camp Pritchard,
Dec. 12th/62

I would not be at all surprised if something did not turn up on the coast sometime soon, as the enemy's vessels are moving about a great deal of late as if they are preparing for something. They are frequently seen going in the direction of Savannah with troops on board and an attack in that direction would not surprise me any day. I keep a man, who was once a sailor, at Foot Point, within 4 or 5 miles of where they anchor their fleet, and send a daily report to Brig Genl Walker, Brig Genl Mercer,[30] Savannah, and to Genl Beauregard of all the movements he reports to me. Anything of importance I telegraph immediately.

I have begun having much stricter discipline since my return than before, which I find much better. Two of Capt A– men are to be tried at Pocotaligo before a Genl Court Martial on next Tuesday (Harrison & Joe McAlbany) for leaving their picket post and I expect it will go very hard with them. Our Asst. Surg. Rivers has been acting very badly of late and if he does not resign I feel bound (and shall do it) to prefer charges against him and have him Court Martialed and he will be cashiered as sure as I do it. He came to me on last Sunday and asked me if I would approve a requisition for 2 gal of whiskey for the use of the Hospital as there were several men needing it very much. I told him I would, if that was the case. So he made out the requisition, which I approved, and went to Hardeeville on Monday in a buggy and got it and got beastly drunk on it. (It was the day I went to Pocotaligo and did not get back until night. He was in bed when I got here, asleep & could not or did not get up for supper). I find today that the whole 2 gal. are gone and none of the sick have taken any of it. I have also found out that he has been doing the like for some time. I hear he says before he will stand the Court Martial he will resign. He has not eaten at the table when I did nor come in speaking distance of me since last Sunday. I have no personal feeling against him, but mean to do my duty.

I hear Dr Rivers is writing out his resignation tonight. If it is not handed in before Monday I shall forward the charges.

*Dr. Rivers, indeed, did "hand in" a letter to Major Stokes, which is reproduced in its entirety and speaks for itself.*

Head Quarters
10th Batt. Cavalry S.C.V.
"Camp Pritchard"
Dec. 13th 1862

Major Wm Stokes
Dear Sir:

I addressed you last night a communication (unofficial) from which I have heard nothing. I take this method of respectfully tendering my position and requesting an answer as soon as convenient. Well hath the "bible" said "Hope deferred maketh the heart sick." You have never known perhaps and I pray you may never know the agony I have endured the past week. The prospect before me is dismal in the extreme. Before a Court Martial though proven innocent disclosures would necessarily be made, which would burn me for a life time with a prospect before me of blasted hope, a disgraced man and very probably a broken hearted wife. You may imagine why I have passed sleepless nights, restless days and the names of food become disgusting. You have those Major in your far off home, for whom your heart yearns and your bosom glows with conjugal and parental love. To whom you would "leave at home, *they too had rather die than shame.*"

Let them though absent speak for me with all the eloquence, all the power their names conjure by our imagination. The chortling (yours) based as they will bestow the surmise and prattling of a talkative community—may well be laid aside altogether. To you I appeal as he who cannot sin was appealed to when "implored." In wrath remember mercy. With regard to the use of Hospital Stores, to which charge alone I would plead guilty, I am willing and will replace them. This much you can grant, that you will lay aside that charge with a guarantee for the future that you will have no foundation for a charge, and while making use of but little (that has been used) myself, I am willing to replace the whole. With regard to the 'Book,' I would assert my innocence not merely before a 'Court Martial' but before the Court of high heaven—As God is my judge I had nothing to do with that loathsome, filthy affair—As far as drunkenness is concerned. My honor is pledged that I was not

59

drunk. Flimsy and uncertain reports are not proofs, but can do what proofs can viz injure and that eternally, the character of any one, hence my objection to and anxiety with regard to a Court Martial. If these charges can be dropped or not preferred, you will have the lifetime gratitude of myself and of a wife and daughter, Ladona. If they cannot be dropped, which with due deference I think can safely be in consistence with duty, will you consent to a transfer, and a resignation alone will do, will you be kind enough to allow that resignation to reach its destination and return. This suspense I cannot endure much longer, excessive worry causing a return of Hemorrhage of the Lungs to which I was once subject. Consider the subject well. And God grant that I may hear from you like the three welcome words "Go and Sin No More."

Very Respectfully
your Obt Servt

/s/ C. M. Rivers

*The next day, Dr. Rivers writes a second letter pertaining to the same subject, reflecting action taken by Major Stokes from the earlier correspondence. It, too, is presented in its entirety.*

Hd. Qrs. 10th Batt
Cavalry S.C.V.
Camp Pritchard,
Dec. 14th 1862

Major W*m* Stokes.
Dear Sir.

Your communication of this date has been received, at the hands of Capt Barber, and the content carefully noted. While I [acknowledge] that a "sense of duty" will not allow you to grant my request, I am obliged for the Courtesy of your address and the opportunity afforded of a resignation, I would have preferred that the subject had been confined to the Battalion and my name not mentioned to outsiders in Connexion with such a subject. Though tramelled and hampered as I am at present, the time may come, nay will come, when regret will take the place of offended dignity, and my name be mentioned in the Battalion with feelings of kindness and a desire for my return. You will lay me under greater obligations Major if you will inform me of the names of those who have made the Reports of which you have spoken.

I am Sir Very Respectfully

/s/C. M. Rivers

Capt Barber will hand you my resignation and application for leave of absence which you will oblige me by approving & forwarding—

*Dr. Rivers' case must wait until a later date to be disposed of. In the meantime, Major Stokes attends to the duties of running his battalion.*

Camp Pritchard
Dec 16th 1862

Should the Government continue to feed the troops of Beef alone I do not know where it will come from in the course of a month from now. The butter was very fine and I want you to ingage some more for me as soon as that is gone. I mean to try to have something to eat if it takes all I make to get it. I have had no flour for some time, but we get along very well without it.

We had a fine review today. Genl Walker sent his Inspt Genl Capt Clark down to inspect us. He was very much pleased with the appearance, drill, etc. He said to me after the Inspection that I ought to feel very proud of such a command. I commanded myself for the first time since I returned and experienced no bad effects from it.[31]

Col Ellis of the 11th Regt at Hardeeville has resigned and his resignation has been accepted. Genl Walker gave him the alternative to resign or be court martialed and he chose the former.

Dr Rivers wrote me two very urgent appeals to consent to his being transferred rather than to be court martialed or resign, but I had to inform him that my sense of my duty as a commanding officer would not allow me to do more for him than to resign, which he did on Sunday night and I forwarded it on Monday, so I hope to get clear of him soon. I have nothing personally against him but I do not want any such man about me. He thanked me for what I did for him, for he knew I had him completely in my power and could have ruined him forever, but I allowed him to get out in the most honorable way possible.

I am making every one toe the mark pretty well and expect soon to have a thoroughly disciplined command. I see the great Battle in Va has been opened. Also in No. Carolina our time may come next.

*The "great Battle" that Major Stokes mentions in his letter of December 16 is as close as his mailbox. A letter from his brother-in-law and fellow officer arrives, giving him a first-hand account of conditions.*

Camp near Fredricksburg, Va
Dec 18th 1862

Dear William.

I received your letter yesterday morning just as we returned from the Battle.

I suppose you know that a Battle has been fought at Fredricksburg. The enemy crossed the Rhappahanack[32] in force on Friday and on Saturday we repulsed them with great Slaughter on their side. Our loss is small compared with theirs. Only two Divisions of our Army were engaged—namely McLain at Fredricksburg and A P Hill ten miles down the River. We were not engaged at all, yet had some killed & wounded in our Brig. by Shell from the enemy. Our Regt lost one man wounded, R A Tinkler, Private Co 'G,' Head wound—Since we were in the Center of Line of Battle and could see the Battle as it raged.

I believe I will close. You must write as soon as convenient and tell me all the news.

I am your Bro Ve [?]

/s/ J. R. Boulware

*Several months had passed since Major Stokes had first heard that his battalion would become part of a new regiment. It was officially formed as the 4th S. C. Cavalry on December 19, 1862. A list of the principal officers and NCO's follows:*

*Colonel B. H. Rutledge, Commanding Officer*
*Field and Staff*
   *Lieutenant Colonel William Stokes[33]*
   *Major W. P. Emanuel*
   *Adjutant G. E. Manigault*
   *Surgeon I. McP. Gregory*
   *Asst. Surgeon Charles Dupont*
   *Quartermaster J. W. McCurry*
   *Commissary A. P. Lining*
   *Sergeant-Major W. A. Benton*
   *Ordnance Sergeant H. G. Sheridan*
   *Coms'y Sergeant G. McD. Cordes*

*The promotion entitled Colonel Stokes to a raise in pay from $162/month to $185/month. On the following day, he provides further details of the new regiment.*

Camp Prichard,
Dec. 20th, 1862

Our Regiment has been formed at last, and I received the appointment last night as Lieut Col. [See Appendix I, No. 6.] The following is the order and letters of the companies composing the Regiment, viz.:

Company  "A",  Capt James C. Craig, of Emanuel's Battalion
            "B",  Osborne Barber,  Stokes' Battalion
            "C",  John C. Calhoun,     "       "
            "D",  Thos. Pinckney,  St. James Mt. Riflemen
            "E",  Henry Edens, Emanuel's Battalion
            "F",  H. Godbold,      "       "
            "G",  Wm. P. Appleby,  Stokes' Battalion
            "H",  John C. Foster,      "       "
           " I",  S. J. Snowden,  Emanuel's Battalion
           " J",  R. H. Colcock,  Charleston Lt. Dragoons

The field officers are Col Rutledge, Lieut Col Stokes; Emanuel, major.

Capt Clark, who was on a tour of inspection, left here this morning, and thinks it quite likely that our whole Regiment may get to Pocataligo. I should be very much pleased to get there.

*Now that the new regiment had been formed, it underwent training, further organization, and inspection.*

Camp Pritchard
Dec 22nd/62

I am very well & go to Charleston tomorrow to appear before the Confederate Court, to show cause why a young man in Capt Barber's Co. under 18 has been detained in service, which I knew nothing about until the writ of *habeas corpus* was served on me from Judge McGrath. It will be something like the suit of Col Blacks and I expect to hold him. I will return on Thursday again.

The enemy's gun boat shelled a good deal at Buchiry [?] Ferry on last Saturday. Some of the shells were filled with bullets. The pickets gathered some two or three hundred of the lead bullets. I carry a portion of the shell to Genl Walker tomorrow at his request and some of the bullets; they are stuck on the inside of the shell with Sulphur and when the shell[s] burst to pieces they fly in every direction.

Mills House, Charleston
Dec 24th 1862

I expect you will be anxious to hear how I came out with my case in the Confederate States Court: The opposite party was not present and Judge McGrath threw it out and they will have to begin anew to bring it up again. The Confederate attorney not being present to represent me in the case, I was introduced to the judge and had a pleasant conversation with him and he instructed me what to do. I found him to be a very pleasant man indeed. I shall return to camp tomorrow. I wish the

64

fellow "had have let it alone" as my fare at the Hotel will cost $8 or $10. My traveling expences will [be] paid by the Government. Everybody thinks an officer gets so much but they never think once what he has to pay out for nothing.

I also added another star to my collar.

Camp Pritchard,
December 28, 1862

Capt Dubois[34] (a Frenchman and good officer sent from Richmond to inspect the Cavalry of this Dept.) is here giving us one of the most thorough inspections I have had since I have been in service. The other inspections did not take more than about half a day and he is taking two days. He inspects everything. Col Rutledge is with me also today. He came down last night and will leave in the morning. He told me that Capt Dubois told him (Col R.) that he was very favorably impressed with my command, both in regard to drill and condition of camp and discipline. Col R. is very much pleased with this portion of the Regiment and we hope to get it together at Pocotalego or Grahamville. General Beauregard[35] has promised to put it together as soon as possible. Still I think it will be a month or two yet and I would not be at all surprised if we get together before the spring.

Camp Pritchard
Dec. 29th 1862

The Captains of this command marched all of their companies round here last night and called on Col Rutledge for a speech, which took all of us by surprise. We did not know [what] they were about until they took their horses after the line was formed. We all went out and the Col made them a short speech, and as soon as he was through they called on me, but [I] excused myself after a few remarks, on account of my cold and a tickling in my throat. Capt Dubois was then called on, who excused himself on account of not speaking English plainly; they then marched off very quietly. Still I did not think it was right as it was Sunday night.

65

From what I can hear of our Regt it will be the finest in the Confederate service and will number about 1.000 men or more. I heard Emanuel's are all large companies. I have over 400 in my command here.

Camp Pritchard,
Dec. 31st/62

I gave a very close inspection today under Genl Beauregard and can make a better report of them than I expected. The companies here were inspected by Capt Smart and mustered for pay. Capt Barber inspected Smart's and Capt Calhoun a Battery of Artillery near here, Capt Earle's,[36] so Capt Appleby had to command the Batt here.

# 1863

★ ★ ★

*The new year changes nothing. Training continues; disciplinary problems, both old and new, remain a constant.*

Camp Pritchard
Jany 4th 1863

Capt Barber is under arrest now for disobeying or rather not carrying out Genl Walker's orders regularly, regarding a daily inspection of his arms etc. Capt Clark who, you will recollect inspected us some time ago[37] asked Capt "B" if he carried out that order and he told him that he inspected *semi*-weekly. When he made his report to Genl W–, the Genl sent me a copy of Clark's report (which was very complimentary with that exception), and asked me why Capt "B" did not make daily inspections as ordered. I made Capt "B" give me his excuse in writing and forwarded it to the Genl which was equivalent to no excuse at all. He immediately ordered me to arrest him and prefer charges against him, which I have done, and I think it will go pretty hard with him, as it shows a great deal of negligence on his part. It is no more than I expected, for I tried him in every way to get him to have discipline in his company.

Lt Rivers has returned and I hear he intends standing his trial before he will forward his resignation again. I mean to prefer them[38] in a day or two more. His resignation was based on ill health and Genl Beauregard sent it back for him to get the certificate of the Sur[geon] on it.

Camp Pritchard,
January 20, 1863

I am moving all of the companies together in front of my quarters and will have one of the best arranged encampments I ever saw. The stables are arranged in a square and the hollow of the square is a lot.

The men under eighteen and over forty years of age have been ordered by the Sect of War[39] to be discharged at the expiration of their term of service and I have discharged them all.

*Union land and naval forces had held the harbor at Port Royal
and its adjacent islands since late 1861. There had been repeated
action to destroy bridges and sever contact between Savannah and
Charleston, i.e., the battles at Pocotaligo, Coosawhatchie, and various raids along the railroad line, though with little success. Intelligence estimates for the beginning of 1863 and throughout the spring
indicated that the enemy still intended a major attack on Charleston or Savannah. The 4th South Carolina Cavalry was being
counted on to assist in beating back the expected assault.*

Camp Pritchard,<br>January 25th, 1863

All is quiet down here now, though the abolition fleet at
Hilton Head is 4 steam frigates (that is large war ships), 4 gun
boats and 40 transports. I heard heavy firing in the direction
of Savannah yesterday, but have not heard the cause. The
Batteries might have been practicing.

Dr. Rivers' trial was ordered to come off on tomorrow, but
it cannot as he is absent and all the witnesses but one. My
whole command lost about 20 men by discharging those
under 18 and over 40 years of age.

Camp Pritchard,<br>Jan. 27th, 1863

Capt Earle & Mikle [?] went to Buckingham Ferry today to
shoot the y– boat with his Battery. A boat soon came along
and they commenced on it but the shots falling short. The
boat then commenced on them and soon made the place too
hot and they ran off without getting anyone injured. I told
Capt E– that would be the result when he was going down.

Camp Pritchard,<br>January 31, 1863

Today the General had a review of all the forces at Pocotalego, consisting of three Regiments of reserves, eight or nine
Companies of Cavalry, two Companies of Artillery and two or
three other Infantry Companies, in all about 2000 or more.

70

The Genral invited Col R. and myself to go out on the review with him and take a position as Staff Officers.

Just as the review was nearly through the dispatch came to the General that our two gun boats had gone out this morning and sunk two of the enemy's gun boats with all on board and badly crippled another which had got off under a flag of truce.

Camp Pritchard,
Feb. 3d, 1863

There have come in to Port Royal since last Sunday 18 Gun boats or rather there that number is there now, 4 Steam Frigates (Large war vessels), and 31 transports. Charleston or Savannah are one or the other to be attacked. I think it is Charleston and believe all they are doing at Savannah is a faint to draw our forces. Our Gun Boats have covered themselves with glory. I am kept busy Telegraphing and giving reports of the Abolition Fleet as they arrive and their different movements. I telegraph Genl Walker and signal Genl Mercer in Savannah through the Signal Corps, which is done by different kinds of flags. Charleston is expected to be attacked on next Saturday or the first of next week. I would like very much to be there.

A number of my officers are absent recruiting. I have ordered them back. Capt A. is not but if I was him I would return immediately, as there is no telling how soon we may be ordered to where active operations are going on.

I continue very well and have not had an attack of Hemorhage since my return to camp.

Camp Pritchard,
February 6, 1863

Nothing of any importance has occurred since I last wrote. The Abolition Fleet is daily increasing. It now numbers (70) seventy vessels (4 Steam Frigates, 13 Gun Boats and 53 transports) that can be seen and I suppose there are others that can not be seen. The above was the report at 5 o'clock P. M. yesterday. By a telegraph from General Walker[40] this evening he requires me to telegraph him twice a day. It is 25 miles from

71

Foot Point where we see them, to Hardeeville.[41]  I have six men (couriers) on this line to bring these dispatches in haste.  My men are being hard worked now, harder than they have ever been, though I hope it will not last long so.

Camp Pritchard,
Feb. 10th, 1863

It is now 10 o'clock P. M. and I have to get up in the morning before day to go to Pocotaligo to attend Capt Barber's trial.  He seems to be in good heart and thinks he will come off clear.  I do not see how he can myself.

The Abolition Fleet is about 78 vessels that can be seen though I suppose there are a number of others.  I think they have about 30.000 troops there at present.  They may attack at Savannah or Charleston soon or wait for the next moon.
It will not be long.  Their pickets do some talking every day at Buckingham Ferry.  They say they are coming to see us soon.  My pickets then ask them if they remember Pocotaligo and told him to go to *hell* etc.

Hardeeville,
Feb. 11th, 1863

I am on my way to Pocotaligo to attend the Courts Martial in Barber's case.

Camp Pritchard,
Feb. 14th, 1863

I am very well, and every thing is working better than I have ever had it since I have been in command.  The rules that I have established for the government of the camp are enforced & everything goes on in military order.  The men are under very good discipline now.

The enemy are quiet down here and their fleet remains about the same (75 vessels).  All are anxiously awaiting the attack.  I do not care how soon it may come, as I am tired of reporting their fleet two or three times a day.

Camp Pritchard,
February 17, 1863

Col Lay of General Beauregard's Staff is here inspecting us.

Camp Pritchard,
February 19, 1863

The Fleet still continues large at Hilton Head. There are about eighty vessels and among them two Iron Clads[42] that are in sight. We are anxious for the attack to come off as we are sure that it will and must come. Our Regiment is to be concentrated at Pocotalego, though a portion of it may go to Green Pond (not Green Pond Church), but I should like very much to command a portion of it at the Church if I know that the enemy would remain where they are. The Green Pond alluded to is, I think thirteen miles from Walterboro. I rather think if a portion of it is sent to Green Pond that I will be put in command of it. I am in hopes all of our Regiment will be kept at Pocotalego. We will move as soon as the necessary arrangements are made, which I suppose will be in 3 or 4 weeks.

Camp Pritchard,
Feb. 22nd, 1863

The Yankee Genls I suppose are still waiting for their rank to be decided before they attack us. I look for them to wait now until the full moon. I wish they would hurry up things and have it over. Col Stephens Regt (24th) is at Pocotaligo. . . . The Col had Capt M. Appleby under arrest, William says for not returning to his Co. as soon as the Legislature adjourned, but I hardly think [that] is it. The Abolition Fleet at Hilton Head that can be seen are 2 Steam Frigates, 19 Gun Boats and 70 transports. They have a pretty large army there now. I suppose 40 or 50.000.

We will move to Pocotaligo as soon as this attack is over. I think Col R wrote me we would soon move there. He wanted me to mess [eat] with him; in fact, he wanted all the commissioned Staff to mess together. He is proud of Col Lay's report of my command here as I am myself. I have taken a

73

great deal of pain in disciplining these Co.; and anyone has a right to be proud of them. I am only sorry now that I had not kept them all the time in our encampment.

Dr Jos. Foster (Capt Foster's brother) the Surgeon of the 5th S. C. regt is here to [see] his Bro. He says Jim[43] is a particular friend of his and that he went to see him just before he left Va. He was well and getting on well. He says his tent and Jim's are near together. I heard this evening that Genl Jackson's Brigade, which has the 5th & 6th in it are on their way to this State. I hope it is so. We want more troops.[44]

Camp Pritchard,
Feb. 24th, 1863

The enemy Fleet has increased some 40 vessels within the past 24 hours. They now number 127 vessels, 20 of which are Gun Boats and 20 large Steamers with only two guns and the remainder transports. A negro scout that Genl Walker had over on Beaufort Island for the past 3 months came over last night under the pretense that he was coming after his wife and says that they intend attacking Pocotaligo and Genisses [?] Pond near Savannah both at the same time, one day this week. He says they have 40,000 Troops with which they intend to attack us. Thank God we are well prepared on the line of R.R. to meet them now. We have a Brigade of 4 Regt of N.C.V. and Col Stephens Regt at Pocotaligo besides the same Troops that we whipped them there with before. We expect to whip them 10 to one if they come now. We have good Batteries on nearly all the roads. There is a good deal of commotion among the y– Troops on the Island today and the attack may come off in a day or two. You must not believe one half [of what] you see in the papers nor what people say Genl B– says, for one half of the time it is lies started by some fellow & then goes for the truth.

I think Col Lay is going to give me justice in his report. He stopped at Pocotaligo on his way to Charleston & Col Rutledge sent me word tonight that he was truly happy to hear the report that Col Lay made of myself and my command. He said Col Lay as good as said it was the best discipline and drill command of cav. in the Dept. I am in hopes Genl Walker will hereafter give me more credit for what I do than he does those that tell him big tales and do little of nothing.

Dr Foster, who had been in Va for two years, said it was the best command he had seen.

*A timely letter from General Stokes' brother-in-law, who had last written from Fredricksburg, relates the status of the war in Virginia.*

Camp near Petersburg, Va
Feb 26th/63

Your last letter to me has just reached me. I also got one from Sallie. I was glad to hear from you & Sallie. Since I wrote to you last I have seen hard times. We had a long march from Fredricksburg to near Petersburg. I think Longstreet's[45] entire Corps is coming down and I think we are simply here to be sent to the place most in need of us—probably to Charleston or Vicksburg—may be down toward Suffolk. It rained & snowed on us all the way down and you may guess the road was bad, over ankle deep every step—and at night we sheltered ourselves as best we can—have not tents etc. Upon our arrival here it snowed to the depth of one foot and is on the ground still—yet we have little or no pneumonia—a good many colds— [unintelligible] all of your acquaintance are well & hearty.

We are expecting to hear of Charleston or Savannah being attacked soon—hear good news from Mr. North but I put no confidence in anything I see in the Papers—I think we must whip the armies in the field and then we can talk Peace.

I see the yankee congress has passed a conscript Bill and they may keep up for some time yet.

I put no confidence in what the Legislature have done or are doing [in] Ky, Illinois, Indiana etc. I do not think any thing of importance can come from it and do think that we had better put more trust in our own arms than in any power north of [the] Mason-Dixon Line. If we can hold *our own* at Vicksburg & Savannah, Charleston & Port Hudson—all will be over in this month's time. Upon such an issue depend[s] an Early Peace.

I spent a day at Drewey's Bluff since I returned from Richmond [the rest is unintelligible].

Your obdt. servt.
[signature unintelligible]

*Notwithstanding the optimistic attitude presented in his brother-in-law's letter, the Abolition Fleet is still as ominous as ever, and looms as a predator of Confederate hopes.*

Camp Pritchard,
Feb 27th 1863

I went down to see the fleet on day before yesterday. They have the river and Bay lined with them for 5 or 6 miles. Such a sight of masts I never saw before. Three came in while I was there. It is a very formidable fleet, but I feel sure they will get whipped. Charleston is undoubtedly the point of attack, but I expect the line of R.R. will be attacked first.

Tomorrow being the last day of the month is a day of general mustering and inspection to pay. I am ordered to muster and inspect Capt W. E. Earle's Battery of Artillery and Capt W. E. Earle, my command. I got the order yesterday evening, which allowed me but a short time to prepare to inspect something I never studied, but I can go through it like a flash now.

The guns you heard the other day were fired from our guns around Savannah while Genl B– was reviewing them and I think were the heaviest I have heard since the war began. They made this whole house shake like an earth quake. Do not let those big guns fret you, for there are more danger in small arms than those big guns.

Camp Pritchard,
March 1st 1863

I have just been reading my Bible until I got tired. . . . I am still very well, but my left arm is pretty sore where I vaccinated myself a few days ago. It looks like it will make a pretty good sore. Dr Rivers[46] had everyone on the lookout by reporting a case of chicken pox, when the fellow who had it had never been vaccinated. It had one good effect. Every fellow wished to be vaccinated. I would not let him vaccinate me. I vaccinated Mike at the same time and his has taken also.

The Fleet off Hilton Head is still large (121 vessels are reported this morning). We are daily looking for an attack and I do not care how soon it comes. If come, it must.

Camp Pritchard,
March 3d, 1863

A battle has been raging at Grimsse [?] Point and vicinity all day I suppose from the incessant bombardment. I look for the attack to be renewed again tomorrow, if the enemy has gained anything by today's work. I would like very much to know what has been done. I do not think we will likely be attacked here, unless it is at Red Bluff. Genl W– looks pretty strong for one there and has ordered me to cooperate with the infantry there to prevent their landing. It is a hard place to defend and should it be attacked there will be bloody work for we mean to do our best, though I do not expect to unnecessarily expose my command.

I was at Hardeeville today on a board of survey on some Quartermaster stores. Genl Clingman's[47] N. C. Brigade passed there going to Savannah. I hear that Genl Longstreet's[48] Corps are coming on here. I hope it is so.

I thought that the bombardment had ceased below Savannah, but I walked out just now and they were firing still every two or three minutes and the moon is bright enough to keep it up all night and load troops and renew the fight with redoubled energy tomorrow. I feel confident that we will whip them though. I have no idea what force we have though. I have been wanting them to commence [for] some time and I am glad to see that they have started.

My health is better now than it has been at any time since I had that attack last fall & I weigh more than I ever recollect of weighing before in my life. I weighed 133 lbs. about a week ago & today I weighed 134 1/2 lbs. so you see that I am improving. I only hope I may continue to improve until I get real hearty again.

*With the imminence of attack, the problem with Dr. Rivers seemed to have been forgotten. Yet, the next letter resurrects it like Jean Valjean's nemesis in* Les Miserables.

Camp Pritchard,<br>Mar 5th, 1863

Genl Beauregard ordered me to order Dr. Rivers to report to Charleston to the Provost Martial in arrest. He leaves tomorrow. I do not know what he will do with him. I had to put the Adj under arrest for conduct prejudicial to military discipline and do not know but that I will have to prefer charges against him. The Fleet that attacked Genasses Point has not returned yet to Hilton Head. There are still some 95 vessels there. All quiet since yesterday.

Camp Pritchard,<br>March 8th, 1863

A great many persons are looking for an early peace. I have always had grave doubts whether it would end before the expiration of Lincoln's term and I am now more fully impressed with that belief than ever, unless there is a perfect revolution and uprising in the North. A great deal depends upon our next and impending battles west and south. We must fight it out ourselves and turn a deaf ear to all talk of foreign intervention.

A few of the vessels that attacked Fort McAllister have returned to Port Royal. The fleet there now is over 100 vessels.

Two scouts of ours were sent over to Hilton Head week before last by Genl Walker, who stayed over for three or four days and reports five Regts of Infantry and one Squadron that they saw, and that they were cutting all the short timber there was on the Island, that the Island was nearly all cleaned up. The same fellow that took that prisoner over there was one of their scouts.

I have released the Adj. from arrest today as he repented of his conduct. The conduct was this: some of the men got vexed with him and put up a price on a tree in camp on him and signed no names to it. He got so mad about [it] that he got his pistol and a shotgun and started out to curse and abuse and shoot he did not know who, and I ordered him to his room in arrest.

Col R– wrote me he would send down the supper of the Regt to me in a few days, also the commissary; he says he wants to gather all the Staff and me until we get together.

Camp Pritchard,
Mar 11th, 1863

I am going to have a fine dinner tomorrow. I have just given $4 for a fine wild turkey Gobbler that one of Capt A– men killed, a big price but I could not get it any cheaper. I wish I was at home with it . . . .

I have my same Adj. yet. He was not relieved, but I wish he was.

Camp Pritchard,
Mar 15th, 1863

You saw the account of the capture of 9 prisoners in Hilton Head by Capt Miklen. I saw them all. The officer was a very intelligent fellow and nothing could be elicited from him or the men, except that we would not have to wait long for the attack. They were sent to Genl Walker. He may get something out of them by surprising them. The Lieut was from N. Y. The others were from Maine. The men say they are tired of the war and do not know who they are fighting for now. They enlisted to fight for the union, but the union was now gone beyond hope. Capt M– intention was to capture all the men stationed at the Signal station and burn the house; he prowled about and spattered turpentine on the house and set it on fire, but they succeeded in putting it out after he left. He brought them down to his boats at the double quick, bare footed & in their drawers some of them. The Lieut got his feet badly scratched by the burrs, but they were all pretty well fixed up when I saw them. They say that Genl Hunter would not believe that we took that fellow off Hilton Head some time ago, that he deserted, that none of our men had ever been over there since the Island was taken, that we were afraid. They have four Iron Clads there now, three of which can be seen from Foot Point, and the other one is out on the coast. Their whole number of vessels there is over a hundred.

Dr. Logan, Chief Surgeon of this Military Dist. inspected my camp yesterday and said that it was in excellent condition, so you see we are being praised on every side. There is nothing like discipline and order in an army. A great many of the men think I have got too strict and some are telling lies on me, but I am raising a name for them and myself. I treat them as kind as ever and do all that I can possibly do for them. At the same time I make them obey orders and know their place. The health of the command was never better than it is now, nor do I think that the men were ever so well satisfied.

Camp Pritchard,
Mar 17th, 1863

The Fleet is about the same.

Camp Pritchard,
March 19th, 1863

Capt Barber is still under arrest. The sentence of the court has not come yet. Col R– has not approved Massey as Adj of the Regt. Genl B ordered him to remain until he was purposely relieved is why he is still with me; he is doing much [better] since I gave him a plain talk and brought him down to his duty.

The Fleet numbers about one hundred & twenty vessels. No one knows their intention.

Camp Pritchard,
March 22d, 1863

The Fleet this evening numbers 135 vessels in all, 121 of which are transports. Surely the enemy will move somewhere soon if they intend to do anything before summer comes on.

I heard a tolerably good sermon today from a Baptist preacher from Pickens Dist., who came down to see Calhoun's Co.

*The daily movement of the fleet is of the utmost importance to Colonel Stokes. The attack, he feels, will be signaled by naval formations rather than his having to receive word from pickets of an actual landing.*

Camp Pritchard,
Mar. 26th, 1863

All the gun boats, 3, one Iron Clad and two others, went out yesterday with a number of transports accompanying, apparently bearing south. I suppose an attack is meditated, possibly on Savannah.

Camp Pritchard,
Mar 29th, 1863

I have had a good deal of complaining. Since last night about 8 o'clock, four Captains, one man, and two surgeons, Capt Howard, Capt Manigault, Capt Elliott, Capt Clark and one of Capt Howard's men, who were looking out for a signal route from Foot Point to the R.R. and came up at the time mentioned and the rain has kept them here today. They will have to remain here until tomorrow. It put me up to all I knew to fix them up comfortable. I did the best I could, and they seem to get along very well.

The attack on Charleston may commence this week though I do not think. There are but 3 gun boats and some 80 transports now off Hilton Head.

The Quartermaster Sergeant Elerby, who by the way was an old school mate of mine at Cokesbury, so we have another acquaintance to our mess.

I believe I told you that the Adj. had left our mess a week or so ago. I have engaged an English sabre for seventy-five dollars.[49] If I like it, it is said to be a very fine thing.

Camp Pritchard,
April 2, 1863

On Tuesday my command was inspected by Capt Barnwell of General W.[alker]'s Staff together with the 47th Ga. Regt and two Companies of the 11th Regt and a Company of Artillery at Capt Smart's Camp about 8 miles from here; being the highest ranking Officer, I had command of the whole. The line was about 300 yds. long.

Camp Pritchard,
April 5th, 1863

No important battles need be expected during the summer months unless they could succeed in taking Charleston, which I do not believe they can do. Their forces now menacing our coast will then be drawn (or the majority of them) to Virginia or the west in which event it may fall to some of our lot to go there too. Camp rumour has it that we are to be ordered to Virginia in General Hampton's[50] Brigade, that General H. has made special application to the President for us.

Camp Pritchard,
April 7th, 1863

We have a stunning view from Charleston and should not be surprised any day to hear that it was attacked. Only 30 of the enemy's vessels are reported at Port Royal this evening, which is about the numbers they had there all last summer. You see what numbers are reported off Charleston by the papers. The majority of the infantry at Pocotaligo have gone to Charleston and I hear the remainder are under orders to march at a moment's notice. Several thousand have gone by Hardeeville from Savannah then—a bloody fight it will be when it does come off, I expect. Those Georgians that have gone by here says they mean to fight in defence of the *good old city* to the *bitter end.* I hear that Genl B– means to defend it to the last, and if forced to abandon it will set fire to the houses and leave them nothing but ruins.

I have commenced drilling the Batt. regularly again & find that they have lost a good deal since I stopped or had to stop on account of my health, but if nothing happens I will soon have them better than ever.

*In the early afternoon of April 7, 1863, Admiral Du Pont launched his attack in Charleston Harbor with the monitor Weehawken at the point and his flagship Ironsides in the center of a single file of ships. The plan of battle was to destroy Fort Sumter.[51] But Fort Moultrie, Batteries Bee and Beauregard on Sullivan's Island, and Battery Wagner, and Cummings Point Battery saw otherwise. It was a brilliant victory of the forts over the much-heralded iron-clads. Colonel Stokes comments on the action near his sector.*

Camp Pritchard,
April 9th, 1863

You saw the account of our glorious victory in Charleston. Today Genl. Walker sent down his artillery and burned a gun boat that had got aground [in the] Coosawhatchie River near Port Royal Ferry. The news [is] cheering from throughout the whole line of sea board. The enemy vessels are coming in to Port Royal Harbor from Charleston. Our Iron Clads and [other] vessels came in this evening, though I do not think they have given it up yet. Still I think every attack will be futile.

Camp Pritchard,
April 12th/63

I am well pleased with the Doctor. He will not let [a] fellow shirk duty from deception like Rivers did.[52]

About half the vessels that left P.[ort] R.[oyal] Harbor have returned, though all transports except one of the crippled Iron Clads. The attack is expected to be renewed at any moment the enemy may get ready. I think they intend to try to run the gun boats by the Fort next time; then some of them will meet a waiting game. It is said by our Genls. that the attack on them has proven beyond a doubt that Charleston cannot be taken by water & that their Iron Clads are not invulnerable as thought.

83

Camp Pritchard,
April 14th/63

You seem to fear the wrath of the yankees much more than any need for, on account of their not succeeding in their attack on Charleston. Let them give vent to their rage. It is what we desire. Their rage is only fueled at any time by fear of advancing against us. . . . They have left Charleston; two of their Iron Clads arrived at P. R. Harbor yesterday evening and one of the injured [?] ones two or three days ago.

*At last, in May, the Regiment receives orders to move. Before taking his command to their new station, Colonel Stokes is ordered to serve on a general-court martial in Charleston from May 7 to May 9. (See Appendix I, No. 1.)*

Camp Pritchard,
May 17th, 1863

The like of flies I do not think I ever saw before as there are here. I will leave this camp in a few days and go down the river.

Camp Pritchard,
May 19, 1863

I have been on the go ever since my return yesterday down below, and today to McPhersonville to see General Walker and Col R. about moving the command, which I am glad to inform you I succeeded in doing. Appleby's and Foster's Companies[53] are to leave here on next Friday the 22nd. inst. and Barber[54] I suppose will be removed in the course of a week. I would go along with the Companies on Friday, but the General told me he wanted me to remain here about 10 days and show them the ropes. Lt Col Johnston of Colcock's Regt is to relieve me. I expect to go up on next Saturday week the 30th inst. so all the letters that will reach me after that time must be directed to Pocotalego. There is no office at McPhersonville. I did not select Appleby's and Foster's Company to go first—the General did it. No one will be left here of the Staff with me, but Dr Dupont, the Asst Surgeon of our Regiment[55] and he will go

84

when I go. I expect we will form an almost new mess at Mc-Phersonville. Two of Maj E.'s[56] command have arrived at McPhersonville and two at Green Pond. The Maj [is] in command of those at Green Pond.

Camp Pritchard,
May 24th/63

I have felt a little lonely since Capt A's Co & Capt F's Co. left. Capt Campbell & Capt Lowery's Co. which take their places arrived here at 12 o'clock yesterday, both large Cos., Capt C's 122 & got here with 60 men, Capt L's 125 & got here with 40 men. The others ran away and went home first. I hear that some of them made as much of the move as if they were going off west.

The news you heard about the evacuation of Charleston I think was only talk by folks in civil life. Genl B– might have said that if either had to be given up, Charleston or Vicksburg, that the former would be of least advantage to us & I agree with him, but it never was thought of being given up without a struggle. All the movements of the enemy there now is a faint, as I have been creditably informed that the reason so many of our infantry was ordered off [by] the President, that he had reliable information that there were not more than 10.000 of the enemy on the whole coast of So. Ca. and we have quite sufficient force here to keep them back. Pay no attention to those fellows at home who do nothing else but try to get up some excitement to scare the poor ladies. I am uneasy about Vicksburg, but hope it will hold out. The loss of Vicksburg will be the greatest slam of the war.

. . . . I get so tired of this place. The flies are awful in the extreme. Nearly everything smells like flies, taste[s] like flies and drink[s] like flies. They have almost completely taken away my appetite from me.

Camp Pritchard,
May 31st, 1863

I will leave here tomorrow evening or Tuesday morning. Col Colcock wrote me that Lt Col Johnston would be here on tomorrow and if he gets here by 12 o'clock I will go as far as Grahamville and stay with Dr Dupont and we will go on [to] McPhersonville the next day.

I have charge of the Post at Hardeeville and am having my horse got to go up there this evening to fix up the mail and attend to what business may be there to attend to and return to camp tonight. . . . I have a ride ahead of me of 8 miles there and 8 back, which ride I have been taking every day for the last two days.

I do not know who I will mess with when I go up, though if Col R– does not invite me to mess with him I expect Dr Dupont and myself will mess alone. I hear that Capt McCrary is messing with Sheridan & Elerbe. I do not care about messing with them again. I only have one knife & fork and one cup and saucer to mess with now, but have a plenty to cook in, so I can eat out of the pot until I can do better. I sent to Savannah for some crockery, but none could be found there to buy.

*Another letter from J. E. Boulware, General Stokes' brother-in-law, brings news of the combat operations from Virginia. It is reproduced in its entirety.*

Camp near Franklin, Va.
June 1st, 1863

Your letter was received several days ago just as we were getting orders to march and I have been somewhat unwell since I came back. But I am now well as ever. Bill, we are nearly run to death down here. We have a long list to keep up and few troops so when a few get up at one point—say 10 or 12 miles distant—we have to go and lay them in the sand several days and probably have to go as far the other side of our camp. We very seldom get to stay in camp in peace for one day and night at a time and to tell the truth our Regt, our Brig. are heartily tired of the business. We do not mind fighting as much as we hate the long dusty marches & we all want to get back to Lee's Army. Genl Jenkins[57] heard yesterday from Longstreet that his Brig. would probably be ordered back to the Rappahannock and we suppose will go with Genl Hand[58] as he has applied for us and ain't none of us wish to go with Pickett.[59]  We do not like the Virginians much better than the yankees.  They are so presuming etc.  We want to go but hate the long march to get there as I suppose we will have to march etc.

I have just got a letter from John Steward.  He told me my wheat is about ready to cut.  I have written to him and told him to save 25 bu. for you.  I suppose you will want it, will you not?  You are nearer home than I am.

Bill, I suppose hard *very hard* fighting has been done before Vicksburg.  We hear at last account that the stench of finding dead bodies of yankees was awful, that Johnston was somewhere in [the] rear—that Vicksburg was holding out barely—I look for something from Old Joe[60] before the thing is ended. And if Vicksburg *holds out* which I hope & trust in God it may, I hardly think Old Abe[61] will get his 400,000 men and if he does not I look for cessation of hostilities between now & next January.  I think Old Lee[62] will attempt to *invade* this summer again but he may probably fight about Manassas or in front of Washington first.  Frank has sent up his papers but has not heard from them yet. He talks of getting you to send up another such paper but I think the other will come yet.  Write to me soon as usual for we may not go and if we do go your letter will be sent on to me.

I remain your Brother-in-law

/s/ J. E. Boulware

*In the continuing effort to take Charleston, the Union land forces, under the command of Major General David Hunter, began making raids up the Combahee River, destroying the property of planters and carrying off their slaves. Hunter was particularly fond of using Negro troops for this purpose; he always kept them under the protection of his gunboats. On June 2, another of these raids took place. Colonel Stokes gives an account of these raids in his letters of early June 1863.*[63]

McPhersonville.
June 3d/63

I was relieved on yesterday evening by Lt Col Johnston about 4 o'clock; the wagons were already packed up and we started for Grahamville that night.

Dr Dupont and myself came in the Buggy and got to Grahamville at 8 o'clock and then away at 11 o'clock. We left Grahamville yesterday morning and when we arrived at Poco-taligo we found all the troops assembling and heard that the y—s had landed at Coosawhatchie Ferry and had burned the flowers on Col Heyward's (formerly of the 11th Regt) planta-tion and on two other plantations and took all of [the] negroes off. I remained at the Depot to render my services if needed from 10 o'clock until 3 when Col R thought I would hardly be needed and if I were he would send for me and I could follow on, and that I had better come on out and fix up my tent, etc. The place they camped in is in the vicinity of Green Pond where Maj Emanuel is in command, twenty-five miles from Pocotaligo. The Genl sent down all the infantry and some cav-alry by the cars in the morning and was driven himself in the evening. Col R– was left in command at the Depot and came back late last night and has not got in yet, so I suppose others have gone on [the] attack.

McPhersonville,
June 4, 1863

The Colonel, myself, Capt (the Commissary) Middleton, the Col's Brother-in-law, and Dr Dupont are messing together. We are encamped on a tolerably high pine ridge.

That raid of the enemies the other day was upon the whole a rather shameful thing for us or rather for Maj Emanuel and his men, though I hear that the General does not attach any blame to him. He knew but little of the country and did the best he could with the small force he had. I do not suppose he was

88

able to take more than 50 men in the fight with one Battery of Artillery. Still, notwithstanding he did all he could, it is humiliating to think that the enemy should come out with negroes (300 or 400) and destroy the amount of property they did destroy (over a million dollars worth) and get off without our knowing whether we had killed the first man or not, though we got several pretty severely wounded on our side. The negroes landed at Field's Point and about one Company of whites landed at Combahee Ferry farther up the river and it was they that burned the houses and took off the negroes. The most of the negroes were forced to go I heard; some got away from them after they started. Emanuel's pickets were hardly instructed when the boats passed up the river in the night. They said they thought they were our boats and did not report them until they saw the enemy landing. Today they have landed at Hunting Island two miles below Bluffton and are burning the village of Bluffton, so Lt Col Johnston has telegraphed. He was engaging them. I hope he may capture them all. I am sorry that I was not there myself. I may hear something more before closing this. If so I will write it. I do not think you need be at all uneasy about Col R. giving me all the work to do, as he talks fair enough about the duties. He proffers to drill one day and me the other and that is more than I expected of him. We will commence drilling on Monday.

McPhersonville,
June 7th/63

All the told news we have here is about the raids at Green Pond and Bluffton and the reports are so conflicting and the most of them so bad that I will not attempt to give them. . . . [A]bout 30 houses in Bluffton have been burned. Everybody is giving it to Johnston & Emanuel. I have through Col R– that Genl W–[alker] intends removing Maj Emanuel from Green Pond and sending me there in consequence of the bad management there the other day; I had much prefer remaining here but I am never let stay long where I desire to stay. It is true it is complimentary, but the place is considered much more sickly than this, and that is a great consideration with me

89

in the present condition of my health; besides I will not [expect] considerations will let him off, which I hope they will, for I do not know of any one that will do as well as I think he will do that we can possibly get just now.

The news from Vicksburg is very good indeed just now and I do sincerely hope she will hold out, which I firmly believe she will. Genl Pemberton has fully restored himself to the confidence of the country, and his fidelity to our cause is not doubted in the least.

McPhersonville,
June 11th, 1863

I expected by this time (12 1/2 o'clock P. M.) to have been within 10 or 15 miles of home, but I unfortunately failed to get the approval of Genl Walker to my leave of absence. I took it to him yesterday morning and he told me he was sorry to refuse me, but that he had something he wanted me to do and requested me to postpone the leave of absence for a while. I told him certainly I could postpone it if he had something he desired me to do. He has not told me yet what he wanted me to do and I cannot imagine what it is unless he means to send me to Green Pond. Col Lay of Genl Beauregard's Staff was here last night and has gone today to Green Pond. He is sent to investigate that affair at that place and the affair at Bluffton where he goes as soon as he returns from Green Pond. I would not be surprised if both Emanuel & Johnston were not [relieved].

Col R– went down to Green Pond today with Col Lay and will not return until tomorrow, so you see I am in command of the Regt.

I saw 25 refugees from Fla. who were brought over by a flag of truce at Port Royal ferry. The most of them were women & children and one or two very old men. They were banished . . . because they would not take the oath [of allegiance]. There were some pretty young ladies among them. I was very sorry for them. They stayed here one night and left the next day on the Savannah train. I hear they brought a good deal of baggage. We got very little information from them as they were closely guarded over there and could not say anything much.

They have three negro Regts over there: 1st S.C., 1st Fla. & 1st Mass—1400 strong which came on there a few days ago.

McPhersonville,
June 12th, 1863

The Fla. refugees I wrote about yesterday were from St. Augustine.

We have breakfast about 8 o'clock generally. Bill of fare generally, hominy, bread, meat and a nice cup of Black Tea. I did not like the Tea at first but like it very well now. For dinner two roast chickens, some vegetables (Garden Beans, Irish Potatoes, Crowder Peas, squashes, and anything of the kind we can get) and Tea at night with a little bread, no meat. Dinner hour [is] 3 o'clock. Tea about 8—. I like it all but the hours.

McPhersonville,
June 14th, 1863

I have gotten no positive order yet, but Col R– was up to the Genl Hd Qrs yesterday and when he came back he told me that it was a fact that I would have to go to Green Pond and that the Genl was on a stand whether to send Capt Appleby's Co or the Charleston Light Dragoons with me, though he thought Capt A's would go. Col Lay I hear will report unfavorably in Maj E's case and a board of investigation will be ordered. I expect to get the order to go to G.[reen]P.[ond] sometime the first of this week. The Col says he told Genl W– that our mess was all fixed up and that he hated very much for me to leave, also that it would be very hard on me and the Genl's reply was that he could not consider that when the good of the service required it, that he (Col R.) could not expect to have his best officer with him all the time. The Col then said, well Genl, if you intend it as a compliment, I have no doubt that Col Stokes will go cheerfully and be contented at Green Pond on his Bacon & hominy.

91

*General Hunter's raiding parties had failed to accomplish much, other than harass the planters, looting their plantations, burning the residences, mills, and barns, and invariably being driven back to the protection of the gunboats lying off shore. As a result, he was relieved of his command and replaced by Brigadier General Q. A. Gillmore who began making plans to attack the fortifications defending Charleston. Colonel Stokes writes of events leading up to Gillmore's vicious siege of Battery Wagner,[64] the action to take Morris and James Islands, and the failure of the Union forces to cut the railroad at Jacksonboro.*

McPhersonville,
June 16, 1863

The general sent for me on Monday morning and informed me that he was having an order issued for me to go down to Green Pond and take command of the troops between the Combahee and the Ashepoo Rivers and gave me his ideas about matters in general there. He also ordered Capt Appleby's Company and the Charleston Light Dragoons down with me and has ordered one of the Companies there up here with Maj Emanuel, so I will have the Cavalry Companies and one Artillery Company with me—a very nice little command.

Green Pond,
June 18, 1863

I arrived here about 2 P. M. this afternoon.
My Head Quarters will be within about two hundrd yards of the Station. The Dragoons are stationed within a short distance of the Station, also by General Walker's order. He had ordered every company under my command where they are to camp, no two together, and I do not like it.

Green Pond,
June 21st., 1863

I have been hard at work ever since I came here trying to organize my command and learn the country. I expect I have ridden over a hundred miles in the last two days, in the saddle

92

from morning until after night. I have visited all the picket stations and the most important points I have to defend. The country below here is beautiful and very rich and the majority of the places are under cultivation and several of them with the owners residing on them. A good many negroes have been moved off since the recent raid and there are still too many here yet for military operations. I think from what I can learn that there was regular communication here previous to the recent raid.

Green Pond,
June 23d, 1863

No news of importance here.

Green Pond,
June 26th, 1863

Mr. Porcher, whom I appointed as clerk, with me from the Dragoons, has received an appointment as Confederate tax Collector and has been discharged; he leaves today.

The mosquitoes are perfectly awful here and I can hardly get any sleep . . . at night.

I hear that an order came a few weeks ago from the War Dept. to Genl B's office, ordering our Regt & Col Colcock's to Va and Genl B– replied that if they would authorize him to give up the whole coast, he could do so; if not he could [not] do without them.

We have two distinguished personages down below here 6 miles, Count & Countess Tedini. The count is Italian (he cannot speak English) and he married a Miss Hutchinson down here. She had sent me several messages & as I was passing yesterday going down with Capt A– we called in to see them, who received us very kindly & took a seat near me and told me she was afraid some of her negroes intended to leave on Saturday night.

Green Pond,
June 28th, 1863

Last night was the time the negroes of Count Tedini were expected to leave. I had a guard out, but they did not attempt it. I received a very complimentary communication from Genl Beauregard on the capture of those negroes the other day. I am very pleased with this place, except that I cannot have any rest at night for the mosquitoes and sand flies, which have me in a perfect fever until I smoke them out of my tent and go to bed. They usually keep out there until morning when they return again, though they are not troublesome after the morning is over during the day unless we have a rain after which they are very troublesome. It has just been raining and they are bothering me very much now. I have my quarters out in the woods where there is a good deal of shrubbery (the best place I could find), and I think I will get clear of them as soon as the shrubbery is cut out, which I hope to get down in a few days.

Maj E. has been ordered up to McPhersonville. I hear his trial is to come off tomorrow before a general courts martial at McPhersonville.

Monday Morning
June 29th, 1863

I leave in a few minutes for a ride down the Ashepoo river and it is very probable I will get a wetting, but I am to meet Capt Walter there, who commands on the other side of the Ashepoo, to make arrangements for signaling each other in case of an attack.

Green Pond,
July 1st, 1863

I have just got back from a 40 or 50 mile ride and am very tired, besides am writing by a light wood fire with the mosquitoes singing round me and must postpone writing more until Friday morning.

94

Green Pond,
July 2nd, 1863

This is the worst place for them [mosquitoes] that I have ever been in the army.

Green Pond,
July 6th, 1863

We have no news here except that about 40 negroes belonging to a Mr. Fripp got off to the yankees on Thursday night—some of the negroes from the same plantation who had gone off previously, I learned on investigation, came up Broad's River, which runs up parallel and quite near [the] Congaree in some place in a flat opposite Fripp's place and dragged a small boat across the marsh between the two Rivers into the Combahee and carried the negroes across in that and landed them in the marsh where they walked across to the flat in the other river where they were out of danger and when they got through dragged the small boat back. The place was 5 miles from any of my pickets. I hear that several of the drivers on the plantation knew they were going to leave and did not give me any notice of it. It is impossible for me to prevent the negroes from getting off unless they were to give me a whole Regt of Cav here and then I expect some would go. The planters are to blame for keeping their negroes here. Genl B– has requested them to take them off. He (Genl B) ought now to order them off as a military necessity—negroes have no business below the R.R. and some are down here without any overseers.

*For the next couple of weeks, Colonel Stokes relates what he knows of the assaults on Battery Wagner, Morris Island, James Island, and the siege of Charleston.*

Green Pond,
July 10th, 1863

A furious bombardment is going on in the direction of Charleston. I hear the guns as plain as if they were in 10 miles of me. I do not suppose they are over 35 or 40. It has been

95

going on incessantly ever since daylight. The guns were so distinct that it woke me and I jumped up and went hurriedly to dressing thinking they had commenced another raid down here on the Ashepoo River. Reinforcements are going in. A long train of troops from Savannah passed here just now. I hope we may do them much worse than before, that a number of them may receive a watery grave. I am just from the Telegraph office. The fight at Charleston has been serious. They are shelling each other. I suppose they mean to try us mostly by land for it will be high water at 2 P. M. when I suppose the Iron Clads will pitch in.

Another train of troops has just passed. I do hope we may be successful.

Green Pond,<br>July 12th, 1863

We are having lively times just now. My whole command is under marching orders to move at a moment's notice. The enemy is making a desperate attempt to take Charleston and have a strong foothold on Morris Island. They have made some three assaults on Battery Wagner, our last fortification on that Island and our brave troops have nobly repulsed them each time with great slaughter. They sent in a flag of truce yesterday evening, requesting permission to bury their dead, and admit a loss of 900 killed and wounded, and 500 prisoners. Our loss, I hear, is about 300 killed, wounded and missing. There has doubtless been fighting there today, but General B[eauregard] has suppressed nearly all the news.

I suppose you have heard of the enemy's raid up the Edisto River. They came up within three miles of the Jacksonboro R. R. Bridge[65] and were repulsed by Capt Walter of the Washington Artillery with a section of his Battery. He is in command between the Edisto and the Ashepoo and has one of Col Aiken's Cavalry Companies beside a section of his Battery. I sent Capt Appleby down with his Company to re-enforce him, but it was all over before he got there. The old planter[66] was badly injured by Capt W.'s Battery and was taken down the river eight or ten miles. I suppose the enemy found she could not remain up long and burned her [the boat the Yankees used to come up the Edisto], so they got pretty well punished, though I suppose they got off with two or three hundred negroes. The Ashepoo is the only river that they have not tried and every one thinks they will try that soon. Then we will have to try our hand.

Green Pond,
July 13th, 1863

Charleston must certainly be passing through a trying ordeal. Cannonading was going on almost incessantly yesterday and I still hear the guns belching forth like thunder. The wires are still down from yesterday's storm. We therefore can get nothing by them. I heard from [a] person that came up on the train last night that Fort Sumpter & Battery Wagner drove back the Iron Clads yesterday. Genl Clingman's Brigade arrived Saturday night and about 4.000 troops passed over this road. I feel hopeful that Charleston will hold out now. Their Flag of truce on Saturday said they were surprised to see us so well prepared. I tried to send you a dispatch by telegraph on Saturday, but the wires were so much employed by official dispatches they would receive no private ones, so here after you need not look for a dispatch from me in such times as it will be by mere chance if I get one off. Genl Walker & I kept the wires busy on last Thursday during that attack on the Edisto. I had to give him all the information he got, which I got by sending over couriers. I received about seven telegrams from him and sent back the same number, he in the office at Pocotaligo & I here, both remain[ing] in the office until 11 o'clock P. M. Last night was the first good night's sleep I have got in three nights.

Green Pond,
July 14th, 1863

I expect you feel anxious about me on account of the strong demonstration of the enemy upon Charleston. I am well and am still here under marching orders, though I do not expect any . . . unless Charleston is taken which I hope will not be the case. I do hope everyone in our sector will do likewise. I sent all of my men that can possibly [be] spared if a number is made up to go down for that action. All in regard to worldly matters depend on the defence of Charleston. We are ruined if it falls. The news has been supressed by Genl B– and no particulars are given to the public. I have learned a good deal by members of the C.[harleston] L.[ight] Dragoons who happen to be in the city and came up. The enemy have Batteries on Folly Island that command the most of Morris Island and they have now unmasked other Batteries on another small Island called Back Island that command Secessionville and a good portion of James Island. If they get the entire possession of Morris Island they will be sure to take Fort Sumpter and after that Charleston and should they get the entire possession of James Island they can shell the city. The only way to meet this advance of the enemy successfully is by the fortifications being constructed or Charleston must fall and with it the whole low country up to the neighborhood of Branchville is my opinion & the opinion of a number of military men that I have conversed with, so you see to save Charleston is to save all of that extent of country. Therefore I do hope no one will think of holding back their hands for one day. Let the people around know this that they may do something. Their crops can be easily finished with their old men and women and they can send off the young men. We have troops enough there now to contend with the enemies if it was not for those Batteries which have been unmasked & the Gun Boats. The thoughts of the fall of Charleston and what will follow it make a man feel awful & melancholy. All is quiet just here. I have orders by Genl W.[alker] to impress[67] negroes & tools to erect a Battery on the Ashepoo & on the Combahee. I have sent out to impress the hands.

I sent Lt O'Hern of the C.[harleston] L.[ight] D.[ragoons] to Charleston day before yesterday. He returned yesterday & tells me that Charleston must certainly fall unless our lines of fortifications are soon completed. . . . Things look gloomy, but I still feel that we will come out all right if everyone will do their duty. If Charleston should fall I will move you[68] & the negroes to Fairfield Dist. I will have plenty of time to do it before they can reach our house. I do hope I will not be under the necessity of doing so.

Green Pond,<br>July 16th, 1863

I have not long returned from the Ashepoo where I am erecting a battery on the River. I have a good many irons in the fire just now. The General has ordered me to build a battery on the Ashepoo and one on the Combahee and has got me chairman of a Board of Investigation, besides the regular duties of my office. I am afraid some of them will not be properly attended to, though I shall do all I can for them all.

I feel a little more cheerful than I did when I last wrote; still I do not know that I have much tidings to make me so, except that we have driven the Abolitionist [Fleet] off James Island at the point of the bay and pursued them again in another assault against Battery Wagner. If Genl B– is furnished the necessary slave labor I think Charleston will be saved yet, and we [will] be saved the trouble and loss of abandoning home.

Green Pond,<br>July 19th, 1863

Today (Sunday) has been a pretty exciting and strenuous day with us. I was hurried up this morning from my bed by a courier from Capt Walker, commanding on the east side of the Ashepoo, informing me that there were four boats lying in the mouth of the Ashepoo. We were soon ready and awaited further reports from my own pickets, expecting every minute to hear of their moving up the River, but they reported nothing unusual. About 11 o'clock Capt Walter reported them landing at Bennett's Point, near the mouth of the River on his side of the River, fifteen miles by the course of the River below my pickets, which are stationed on the lower point of [the] mainland on this side. I informed General W.[alker] of the above fact and ordered one section of Artillery (two guns) and a Company of Cavalry to man my lowest Battery on the River. The General telegraphed me that he was coming on a train with a Battery (four guns) of Artillery and two Companies of Cavalry and for me to have one Company ready to go with him on the train to Jacksonboro. I ordered Company "K", C. L. D. to go. He got here about three P. M. and took them on board and off they went, saying to me that my command left was small, but to do the best I could if they came out on this side. The few that had landed had gone back before he got there and the train returning with them passed here about an hour ago, nine o'clock, dropping the C. L. D.'s as they passed. There are still three of the enemy's boats lying in the mouth of the Ashepoo, below Bennett's Point, and we may have a demonstration any time up either the A. or Edisto River. Charleston is having a pretty severe time of it. Several gun boats and the Iron Clads shelled Battery Wagner all day Saturday furiously and on Saturday night they made three desperate assaults with Infantry and were repulsed with great slaughter. Some of them even got into the Fort. The negroes were put in front. I expect you will hear the particulars by tomorrow's paper.

Green Pond,<br/>July 20th, 1863

There was heavy cannonading in the direction of Charleston again last night. Those fellows seem to have taken up Grant's plan at Vicksburg and are sticking to it like death to a dead horse, but I do hope they will not prove successful, as they have not so far. They seem to be displaying an unusual amount of energy. Their charge on Saturday night was a brave one.

Green Pond,<br/>July 21st/63

All is quiet here just now. The yankees are still bombarding *Battery Wagner* every day: *noble little fort.* I hope it will continue to hold out and do as well as it has for an indefinite period. I heard that after that desperate charge of theirs on Saturday night, our Genl in command on Morris Island,[69] ordered a charge, which is said would have cleared the Island, but two N. C. Regts refused to charge. They have since been

100

removed from that Island to Sullivan's Island and some of our *S. C. Troops* have taken their places. Colquit's Brigade is some of *Old Stonewall Jackson's Command*. They say they got at it just right.

Green Pond,
July 22nd, 1863

[I] do not think you need feel any uneasiness about your letters falling into others' hands or about C[harleston]'s fall. It will be two weeks before they could occupy the city. I feel more hopeful than ever now of Charleston from what I have heard today from there.

Green Pond,
July 23d/63

The only news from Charleston is that the enemy still continues to bombard the Battery Wagner. My greatest wish is that she may continue to hold her own as long as they may hammer at her, as well as she has done, so far. If the necessary labor is got and the proper energy devoted to the defence of the good old city, she may yet be saved. Too much speculation in Blockade running among our officers, of high and low grade (I do not allude to Genl B–) in and around the city, I fear, has caused the defences around the same to be so incomplete, and the enemy to catch us in the fix we have been caught in. I hear that Brig Genl Riply[70] has made a great deal of money in that way, also Brig Genl Jordan.[71] The A. A. G. [Assistant Adjutant General] of Genl B– has been at it, and any quantity of lower grade officers.

I received a telegram today stating that the enemy had landed at Point Berry on the Ponpon River seven miles from Adams River this morning & were met by our cavalry and repulsed or rather driven back. I am looking every day for them to give me a round, but they may pop around me all the time.

101

Green Pond,
July 24th, 1863

There was heavy firing going on at Charleston this morning but has ceased now.

Green Pond,
July 25th, 1863

My command was increased yesterday evening by one Co. of Infantry & two siege rifled guns, which Genl Walker sent me. After we get them in position I think we can sink any Gun boat short of an Iron Clad that comes.

Green Pond,
July 28th/63

There is but little fighting going on at Charleston just now or for the past few days, but both parties are busy digging sand.
All is quiet here around Green Pond, though we may have a round any time. I have sent down my two rifled guns on the two rivers and am tolerably well prepared for them if they come high enough on either of the rivers.

Green Pond,
Aug. 4th/63

There has been very heavy firing in the direction of Charleston all night and it is still going on this evening. We hear very little of the particulars from there now. Some say we are getting better prepared for their attack.

Green Pond,
Aug 6th, 1863

The health of the command is much better than it was two weeks ago. We have certainly had a great deal of sickness in Co "F" (Lt Hewett's), one of Emanuel's and the Co. of Artillery. There has not been a great deal in any of the others. I take four gr. Quinine every night & I believe it was just the trick that I needed is why I have fattened up. All of the men in the Co. are required to take 4 gr. of Quinine a day. When it was first commenced here 8 of Appleby's men refused to take it & the Dr reported this to me. I immediately ordered [that] Appleby give them another chance to take it & if they still refuse to do so, to arrest them and send them to the garrison Guard house at McPhersonville and turn them over to the Provost Martial of the Mil Dist. & prefer charges against them for disobedience of orders. When they heard the alternative he told me the Quinine was taken in a hurry. He said that 8 or 10 others said they were [persuaded] to see how those fellows came out.

Matters at Charleston are decidedly better than they were. The general impression now is that if the yankees do not overpower us by reinforcements that Morris Island cannot be taken. The y[ankees] have a line of fortifications clear across the Island parallel with ours (Battery Wagner, which runs clear across). We have several more very heavy guns mounted in Wagner and all together it is a much hard[er] nut to crack than it was. Some of the small guns were taken from the lower tier in Fort Sumpter in order to strengthen the Fort; besides they were where they could not be used. The fort has been greatly strengthened in that way. If Wagner is taken, I think as many of our best guns as can be gotten off will be taken away & the Fort blown.

Green Pond,
August 7th/63

The last three or four days I think were as hot as I ever felt. What an awful time the poor soldiers must have on Morris Island. The glare from the white sand must be enough to blind them. There is one consolation: our enemies are getting the benefit of it also.

Green Pond,
August 11th, 1863

Genl Evans[72] is in Savannah with his Brigade, so you see we are being reinforced with fine troops. I have heard nothing of importance from Charleston recently. All is quiet and hard at work I expect.

Robt Jaques, poor fellow, was accidentally killed last Sunday. It seems there was a chinaberry tree at the post that they had a board in to sit on as a lookout and Wm. McShany was up in the tree and Bob J. & some of the other pickets got to teasing him by chunking at him and after they got through with their play, Bob went and sat down under the tree by the root, working with his gun, when Wm Mc said he had a good mind to let the board fall on him & Bob told him to let it fall, [that] it could not hit him, where upon he let it go. It struck him on the head & he died in about 7 or 8 hours after; I suppose it broke his head. Wm Mc they said took it awful hard. His [Bob's] body was taken home for burial.

Green Pond,
August 13th/63

I am glad to see you in such good heart about Charleston. It may never be taken, but I would not be surprised if you did not receive before long the harmful intelligence that Fort Sumpter is breached and abandoned but that should not dishearten us in the defence of Charleston. Fort Moultrie & Battery Bee on Sullivan's Island still command the entrance. I saw the Hon. Wm F. Colcock this morning from Charleston and he told me that six shells were thrown into Sumpter yesterday, five of which exploded, doing no damage.

We had a little false alarm here last night on the Combahee by some of Genl Walker's pickets shooting at nothing for a boat.

Green Pond,
August 14th/63

I am glad to see you so hopeful about Charleston. The bombardment continues everyday & night. I am very much afraid we will have bad news from Fort Sumpter before many days, as it has been prooven that a brick Fort cannot stand continual bombardment by heavy guns, however strong it may be built. Still I feel it will make an honorable defence.

I heard that Jenkins Brigade was in Wilmington, N. C. awaiting orders so I suppose they will come as soon as [they can].

Green Pond,<br>August 17th/63

No news of importance from Charleston except the same old thing: heavy firing constantly. I heard we passed a night beating off the guns over there this morning from James Island.

Green Pond,<br>August 23d/63

From what I can learn Sumpter is still terrible. It is true the side running to the yankee works is battered down and the Guns on that side all silenced, but it seems that no more damage can be done to that side by the y[ankees] and the sand bags etc. that we had placed in that side formed a considerable defencive position. They may be able by hammering at it long enough to knock down all the back work that is fronting them broadside, but if the Island side remains uninjured and [unintelligible], I do not see why it should not still continue to command the channel. The shell and shot fired into the city Saturday morning I understand, is generally believed to have been shot from Fort Johnston, and that Genl Beauregard had it done in order to run the non-combatants out of the city,[73] which if he did acted like a clown, for they say the city was in a perfect uproar and every cart, coach, wagon etc. was brought into requisition to get to the cars[74] to get off. Another report is that a y[ankee] gunboat must have slipped up near Cummings Point and fired theirs and [gone] back. The y[ankees] lay fire about 1 o'clock a.m. Saturday night and no one knows where from. I rather think Genl B. had it done. You know I said the y[ankee] Batteries could not reach the city.

105

Green Pond,
August 25, 1863

Capt Colcock of the C.[harleston] L.[ight] D.[ragoons] came up yesterday to take down all of his tents to Charleston, which he left standing when he went down. He does not think they will let his Co. return during the siege, which no one knows how long [it] will last. The report about Genl B. having those shells thrown into the city is false. They were thrown from the same Battery that was reducing Fort Sumpter a distance of about 6 miles into the city. It is a novel thing to think that a city can be shelled 6 miles. Little or no damage has been done to the city as yet.

I also heard that we have built a second Battery inside of Fort Sumpter, which is called Fort Sumpter's baby. My opinion is that time alone will tell whether Charleston is to stand or fall. No one knows now.

I have just learned by passengers [from the train] that tell the guns at Fort Sumpter have been dismounted except one mounted in the Sand Battery inside; that the artillery is to be taken out and that the Fort is to be held with rifles, so infantry is to be put in the Fort. Sumpter certainly has been nobly defended with but little sacrifice of life.

*A letter to Colonel Stokes from a certain E. Haueston, serving in Charleston, arrives and gives detailed information on its defenses, morale, and the siege of the city.*

Charleston,
Aug. 30, 1863

We are encamped on the Race Course with everything still in confusion. Our duty is also more than we have ever had to do before. 18 men everyday to guard the Bridge and 10 on Morris Island as couriers. These last go for 5 days and a hard & dangerous time they have of it. Our men are on duty every other day so they have not much rest. We would all a thousand times prefer being with you at Green Pond but as long as this Siege lasts we will certainly be kept here.

106

We still hold Sumpter & Wagner though Sumpter is a mass of ruins and has only two guns that can be used. And the yankees have taken our rifle frets[75] in front of Wagner and still hold them. And I do not [know] if we will even be able to drive them out. They are so near Wagner that their sharp shooters can with ease pick off our men while loading the Cannon making it a very uncomfortable place to be in, but we still hold these places and will continue to do so as long as possible. How long that will be I can't say. Charleston however is not lost by losing Morris Island and Sumpter. There must be some very hard fighting after that. The enemy have once or twice shelled the city—but have not done so for the last four nights. It is reported that we have destroyed the Battery they used for this purpose, and it looks like it. One of the (*Big English*) guns has arrived. They are now at work putting it in place, *"on the Battery"* (*in the city*). It is immense beyond anything we imagined. I do believe that it can send a bolt[76] through the turret of a Monitor at a mile. The bolt weighs 656 lbs. The Carriage[77] is all of iron & I hear gun & carriage together weigh 60 odd tons. The Yankees have nothing to equal it and I do hope these guns may yet save Charleston. We certainly expect much from them, and after seeing, I can believe almost anything I hear of it.

It is doubtful whether the other will be allowed to come to Charleston or not. Beauregard is trying hard to get it.

There is very heavy firing going on now at Morris & James Islands, but I have not heard what it is about.

I suppose you have heard that Gilmer (the Engineer)[78] has been made Maj Genl and put over Ripley. It is said that Ripley[79] has sent on his resignation, but I can't say if true.

The "Segar Boat" which was to do such wonders sunk yesterday & drowned five men, but I believe it was owing to mismanagement and that the boat will be saved and given another trial but doubt if it ever does any damage to the enemy. Still there is nothing like trying.

The lower front of the City is almost entirely deserted: post office, Banks etc. all moved up town to get out of the way of shells. The morning after shelling of the City, I think thousands of women & children & many men left. It did more to get the non-combatants away than anything Beauregard could do & in this way helped us. I have heard no talk about giving up. People seem determined to fight to the last & burn the City if necessary. I hope they will stick to this to the last.

Evans'[80] Brigade has arrived here and Jenkins'[81] is in North Carolina & can be brought on in a very short time. I believe we can get troops enough. So far the Yankees beat us in guns. We had nothing to put against them. 2 & 300 lbs. Parrot guns, but these new Chaps I hope will give us some of the advantage.

It is almost as difficult to hear truly what is going on as it is in Green Pond, but whenever I hear anything interesting that I know to be true, will write to you. I am kept going most of the time being on duty two days out of three.

Green Pond,
Sept 1st/63

We had our bi-monthly inspection on yesterday evening for the pay of the troops. I gathered them all together and commanded myself. All did very well except my artillery Co. It did not do so well. It is quite cold & has been so for several days, rather an unusual August. I like this cold and would be glad for it to continue so. I will have my chimney put to my house very soon if it continues so.

One of the Big Guns is being put in position in the battery in Charleston, which will not do any good until the enemy get clear in. I do not know when the other will be put [in]. I think it ought to be put in Battery Bee. I get but little news from Charleston except what we get by the papers.

*A letter from J. E. Boulware, General Stokes' brother-in-law, arrives from his post, "Camp near Petersburg, Va.," dated "Sept. 4th, 1863." It tells of the war north of Stokes' position.*

I keep well and hearty. The Sickness in our Regt is smartly on the decrease. When I came back the sick list was 160. Now it is 27. We are sitting still at Petersburg. Now and then we run to Richmond & other places whenever a raid or something

108

of the kind is expected. I am glad to know that Sumpter in her shattered condition is more than a match for the yankee host. I am beginning to think that we may be able to beat off Gilmore (the yankee Genl) and cause him to retire in disgust. We put every confidence in Genl Beauregard and feel safe in trusting our Queen City[82] in his hands. We hear nothing from Lee's army—but suppose they are standing still.

Green Pond,
Sept 5th/63

There has been heavy cannonading going on in the direction of Charleston nearly all night and is still kept up this morning. It may be our Batteries.

I suppose the fainthearted people are satisfied that the fall or disablement of Fort Sumpter was not the material consequence that the Enemies' fleet should come in. Sumpter stood like a lamb the other night and took all that the enemy could bring against her without being able to open her mouth. *Noble Fort.*

Everyone is in good spirits just now and I hope nothing will turn up to change the feeling.

Green Pond,
Sept. 7th, 1863

You will doubtlessly hear of the evacuation of Morris Island before this reaches you, at which I hope our people will not be panic-stricken as they were some time ago. The Island was held this long principally on account of Fort Sumpter and to give us [a] chance to get our batteries built on James Island; now that Sumpter is battered down and I suppose our batteries arranged on James Island, it can certainly be of no use to us and but very little to the enemy inasmuch as it only allows them to get a quarter of a mile nearer the city than they were before. It is true we have lost several valuable guns. That is a new item to us. I do not know how many. The enemy captured the last Barge that was leaving the Battery this morning with about 3 men in it at daylight. The retreat must have been well con-

109

ducted or we would have certainly lost more men. They assaulted the Battery just as that last barge was leaving and to their surprise I suppose found it empty. They then marched in playing "Dixie" and cheering. I am in hopes they will have to make much of that and not be able to get a foothold anywhere else. I consider the moral effect of losing Morris Island may be more than the real loss.

I am invited to dine today with the Count & Countess Tedini and expect to avail myself of the invitation.[83]

I heard that Pres– Davis telegraphed to Genl Beauregard that our Iron Clad from England would be into Charleston on the 14th or 15th inst and to hold Fort Sumpter. If it will only *prove true*, what an *auspicious moment* they will arrive.

*Even the siege of Charleston does not take precedence over the other topic that has held man's fancy throughout history: Love, the equal of War, occupying the two major themes of literature. One of General Stokes' officers, Captain Appleby, has been "courting" his daughter Sallie. He comments on this in his next letter.*

Green Pond,
Sept 9th, 1863

Capt A– seemed greatly disappointed in his visit; in fact, I heard him say to someone in my presence, who were teasing [him], "that he went home on purpose to see a young lady, but failed to see her." So you see that my suspicions were pretty correct. I will tell you of another suspicion of mine, but do not desire you to reveal it to Sallie; it is that Sallie will receive a letter from him soon. It is all suspicion on my part, for he has never said anything to me on the subject.

We got some good news from Charleston this morning by telegraph, though I suppose you will get it by tomorrow's papers. The enemy attacked Fort Sumpter in Barges, supposed to be 4.000 strong. 202 were taken prisoner, 10 of which were officers (one said to be Genl Meade's[84] son). One of our gun boats were lying close [unintelligible] Sumpter with shell and grape and it is thought we killed, divided, and wounded a great many. Our men in the Fort fired on them with their rifles and

threw brickbats and hand grenades at them. Maj Stephen
Elliott was in command of the Fort. A cooler or braver man
could not be put there.

Green Pond,
Sept 11th, 1863

I heard a little bad news tonight that our big gun in Charleston busted at the first trial fire. It is true I suppose. It came by
telegraph.

*Although the siege of Battery Wagner had ended on September 6,
Colonel Stokes maintained his defensive positions as additional
action was expected in his vicinity. He remained in command
until early January 1864.*

Green Pond,
Sept 15th, 1863

I have just got off my horse from a long expedition to
[unintelligible] Island where I have been out in command of a
party of eighty men for the past 24 hours with almost nothing
to eat. I am used up to speak it in [a] few words . . . .
At three o'clock Saturday the R.R. agent came running to my
quarters and told me that Mr. Burckhalter wanted to see me,
that the yankees were within a mile of the depot and had cut
the telegraph wire. I immediately raised out my troops and
went in pursuit of them, had them perfectly surrounded that
evening, but 3 of my pickets from Capt Leadbetter's Co. 11
Regt S.C.V. allowed them eleven in number, the Operator, one
1st Lt of 1st S. C. negro Regt and the Chaplain of said Regt
(who came in command of the party) and eight negroes [to
pass]. Night stopped our pursuit on Saturday after they were
allowed to pass those pickets, without either being shot at or
halted. I shall have them punished about 12 o'clock Sunday
after pursuing them [the enemy] about 15 miles in all. I caught
their Chaplain, the Lt, and one negro. I have since caught
another negro and one of their pilots that ran off from Col
H. C. Heywood in that Combahee raid[85]—all of them dressed

111

in uniform. The negro that I captured told me that there were a negro Co. on [unintelligible] Island and I got this expedition up hurredly to capture them as it was a small Island but it looked as if they evacuated on yesterday. They were evidently there. The way I had to get them, we had to walk about 4 miles across a marsh and decidedly the worst place to travel I ever tried in my life & I am worn out getting little or no sleep and nothing to eat for the past 24 hours. I am well with that exception and if this does not make me sick, I will think I am pretty tough.

Green Pond,
Sept 22nd, 1863

I arrived here safe on Sunday evening about 7 o'clock and found things going on very well. Another one of the negroes that came over with the yankee party (the main pilot) was caught during my absence, and through him they were able to procure four good muskets, two Sharps[86] (fine) rifles, one [unintelligible] revolver and a fine opera glass. Appleby has the pistol and I have the glass, though the fellow who found them (Jack Lynes of Appleby's Co.) wants us to pay $50 each for them. They would bring that money but I do not think the glass will be worth that much to me. Capt A– upon impulse of the moment offered him that for them as soon as he found them, which was wrong. 20 or $25. would have been a sufficient reward for finding them. The little Sharps rifle shoots a cartridge like that little four barrel pocket Pistol I had and will be of but little use to us, as I do not suppose the cartridge can be got. I mean to try to keep one for me to have after the war is over if I live to get out.

*Also on September 22, a Letter of Commendation is forwarded from the Commanding General, W. S. Walker, of the Third Military District in McPhersonville, attesting to Colonel Stokes' "untiring energy and skill which resulted in the capture of a portion of the telegraph party of the enemy." (See Appendix I, No. 7.)*

Green Pond,
Sept 23d 1863

I have been offered $100. for my opera Glass, so I think I had better hold on to it.

Green Pond,
Sept 23d 1863

Desertion in the face of the enemy are punishable with death, so those who mean to desert had better think before they act, or they may not only disgrace themselves but their families. I have never been despondent of our cause or of the defence of our city, but mean if the worse should come to try to be prepared. Which I think is the duty of every man where we have such a ruthless enemy to contend with as we have.

The enemy made a desperate attack upon us with the Iron Clads on night before last at Charleston with the supposed intention of reaching our obstructions and passing into the harbor, but were successfully repulsed and driven back without accomplishing anything as far as I can learn. It is said to be the heaviest bombardment of this siege.

Green Pond,
Sept. 29, 1863

Capt Bomar's Artillery Company has been ordered off since I wrote you last and Capt Earle's Artillery Company sent here in his place. Another Cavalry Company (Capt Davis of Jeffords' old command) from Charleston are on their way to report to me, so my command will be increased two Companies. It is rumoured also that the C. L. D.'s will be ordered here in a few days. Capt Davis' Company is sent here direct by General Beauregard. He may possibly think from the enemy sending out their telegraphic party here that they may intend some other movement against this point and he saw from my report that I was very weak.

Green Pond,
Oct 2nd 1863

I look for the enemy to open on Charleston or its surroundings in earnest next week, but I believe all of the officials think
it safe, tho[ugh] all agree that the city may be burned.

Green Pond,
Oct 6th, 1863

I have received my pay for last month and have some to send
home, though not a great deal as I have to pay for that opera
Glass out of it.

Green Pond,
Oct 8th/63

I am going off this morning down the Combahee on a
reconnoitering expedition as soon as I get my breakfast, to
ascertain the place where those yankees came across it, in order
to place a water picket at that point. That was a daring act of
Lt Glassell in trying to blow up the Iron Sides. All is quiet
here. My dog company is having a little chase this morning
after a camp negro who stole something and ran off.

Green Pond,
Oct 9th, 1863

I got through with my reconnaissance . . . yesterday very well
and accomplished what I desired. I found where the enemy
had had a picket post in the Combahee River during the short
period they occupied Willerman's Island where I went on that
expedition to and got a good deal of general information about
the river. I got back to camp about 5 o'clock safe but very
much fatigued, but am feeling very well this morning. The
chase with the negro dog at a boy from Appleby's camp was
successful. They took him after running him about 5 miles.
It has completely taken the negroes down about here and will
have a wholesome effect.

Green Pond,
Oct 11th, 1863

Capt Appleby has two cases of Small Pox in his Co. which he has isolated, but I am afraid it will go through it. It is in nearly all the plantations around here.

Green Pond,
Oct 26th, 1863

. . . [N]o demonstration has been made as yet on the coast, nor does the sign indicate one immediately, still, I would not be surprised if the enemy did not move in some direction this week, though it is not known when. One or two of the enemy's boats came up near Mackey's Point on Saturday. That is where they landed when we had that Pocotaligo fight last year. Genl Beauregard telegraphed Genl Walker on Friday that the enemy was moving south and to look out, whereupon he immediately had me telegraphed for. I think the excitement is based on nothing more and the Genl might have let me take out my furlough. The enemy may attack Savannah or make a feint against it. The Fleet has increased about 25 or 30 vessels at Port Royal.

Green Pond,
Oct 28th, 1863

It was reported yesterday that the enemy had commenced shelling the city, but I think they only threw one shell into the city.

The enemy threw one shell in the city, fired four others which fell short; the gun busted at the fifth shot. Sumpter & Moultrie are being severely shelled. The roar of the cannon is very distinct as I write. All is quiet here as yet.

Green Pond,
Nov 1st, 1863

. . . Pres[ident] Davis passes here between 9 & 10 o'clock and besides being busy otherwise, I will have to fire a national salute of 13 guns on his arrival with Earle's Battery. He was to have passed at 5 P. M. today and any quantity of ladies were out at the different Stations (Hardeeville, Grahamville, Pocotaligo and a few also at Green Pond) to see that high personage and were disappointed.

I heard this evening by telegraph that the bombardment of Fort Sumpter was furious and I am afraid if they continue they will get possession of it. The weather has turned very warm again though I think it will rain in a day or two and we will have more cold.

. . . the Pres[ident] has passed. I commenced firing the salute as soon as the train got within two hundred yds of the Depot and fired thirteen guns. The Pres[ident] as soon as the train stopped sent for me and Genl Gilmer[87] met me and introduced me to the Pres[ident] who said he was very much pressed for time and did not want to come out, but I told him that the ladies who were on the platform would be greatly disappointed and insisted on his coming out when he acquiesced and came out and I introduced him to them and they presented him with some bouquets. He bowed to all and immediately returned to the train and left. I like his looks very much and I think he was pleased with our reception.

Green Pond,
Nov 6th, 1863

I have heard nothing further that our Regt would be sent off. Genl Walker moved his Hd. Qts. back to Pocotaligo on yesterday.

Green Pond,
November 8th, 1863

General Walker wrote me a few days ago that he heard that one of the negroes that I caught with the telegraphic party said that the telegraph apparatus was left somewhere near Lowndes'. I had it hunted and J. D. Carter of Appleby's Company found it today. It is a very fine instrument. We fixed it up in a few minutes and sent a dispatch on it to General W. informing him that it was found. I will send it tomorrow to Pocotalego.

*Writing from Pocotaligo, Colonel Rutledge sends a letter to Colonel Stokes that from its contents is not totally clear, although its tone is consistent with the "officially correct" but testy relationship which seems to exist between the distant leader and the actual commander of the Regiment. It is here included because this out-of-context document does represent a "shard" of the combat record of the 4th South Carolina Cavalry.*

Pocotaligo
Nov. 12, 1863

My Dear Col.

I received your letter yesterday, but altho. extremely complimentary, it was not *satisfactory* to me. I wrote you simply and intentionally a nice official document stating Lieut Nasser's views[88] & asking for your consent or not. You are the *only* person to judge whether you *will* consent or not. You know all about the matter from the beginning, and you know what the word of Hines will require in witnesses etc.—What the examination of the board contemplates may result in, I know not & can not see beforehand. There might be complications under such circumstances. I decline *acting* on my judgment, *for you*, in the affair. I wrote to you Lieut Nasser's request on the board, and if you approve say so to me officially; if not say so with or without reasons and I insist upon the agreement between you which induced your consent to the suspencion of the proceedings.

By the way a piece of business—Is there a "W. Hampton" of Williamsburg Dist Co. F who has *deserted*, or a "W. Hampton" of Co. F of any District or *what* Dist. who is a deserter—

There is news here that the enemy are organizing a strong expedition to attack Ashepoo—Keep your eyes open—

Answer this by return mail—

Yours very truly

/s/B. H. Rutledge

Green Pond,
Nov. 12th/63

The report now is that we will be sure not to go, that a requisition was made by Genl Butler[89] for three Regts. from the coast and was approved by all of the Division and Corps Commanders out there, through which it passed to the War Dept. and the War Dept. sent it to Genl Beauregard for his remarks which were "that if one company of cavalry was taken from the coast that the service would be injured thereby." I got a letter from Jim[90] yesterday. They were at the Depot awaiting the train to go to East Tennessee. Longstreet's whole Corps has gone in order to make a flank movement against Thomas[91] or to operate against Burnside.[92]

A very intelligent negro came over from the yankees to some of Genl Walker's men a few days ago and informed him that the enemy are getting prepared [unintelligible] for an expedition to come out and take possession of this neck between the Combahee & Ashepoo and try to hold it. I do not know what truth there is in the rumor, but it is decidedly the best place for such a thing that I know of on the whole coast of Carolina.

I got the yankee telegraph party's valise yesterday. It and nearly all of the contents were rotten, which consists of about 200 envelopes, 4 grs. of dispatch paper, a good pair of new broad cloth pants and some shirts and two candles, one of which I am now writing by and about the only thing that did not spoil. The pants are tolerably good. They were never worn.

*Hostile action continued along the coast with an engagement against Union monitors at Sullivan's Island on November 16, and boat demonstrations against Fort Sumter on November 19-20.*

Green Pond,
November 16, 1863

Col Anderson[93] commanding the 5th. Georgia Cavalry staid here night before last with his Regiment on their way to Adams Run. He has an excellent Regiment and I think he is a good officer.

Green Pond,
Nov. 19, 1863

Genl Walker has ordered all the camps moved about six miles below here as soon as possible for the winter. I have written him to know if he desires me also to move my Hd. Qrs. and I expect an answer by tomorrow.

Green Pond,
Nov. 23rd, 1863

I suppose you are aware that the enemy is shelling the city daily now, but doing comparatively little damage. But very few of the shells burst. One old negro woman has been killed and an old negro man wounded is all the casualties that I have heard of. The shells have entered several houses. I hear that up to this morning 102 Shells had been thrown into the city. It certainly shows weakness on the part of the enemy; by the shelling of Charleston is virtually acknowledging that they cannot take it and that they mean to try to destroy it with long range guns. I hear that whenever the shelling of the city commences everyone or nearly everyone that is *down* town *finds* some business to take them *up* town, so that *up* town has gotten very popular of late. Those shells are anything but pleasant to the city gentlemen.

Green Pond,
November 27, 1863

They had rather a bad affair at Pocotalego on Monday night. Five Yankees came over with about 30 negroes, reconnoitered General W.'s Head Quarters and got away from them without a man being taken and took with them 20 negroes belonging to Mr. Daniel Heyward. They captured two of our pickets from Calhoun's Company[94] on the Pocotalego River as they were going back, one of whom got away while Col R. was skirmishing with them, with some of his men. They took the other off. We got three or four men pretty badly wounded, of Foster's Company in the skirmish. Some of the enemy were captured. Col R. did the best he could, but it was dark and he could not tell where the enemy had gone.

119

Green Pond,
December 2, 1863

I have just learned that the following dispatch passed over the wire from General Beauregard to Col A. J. Gonzales, Chief of the Artillery, by which it seems that some changes will be made, in which case I will very likely be sent back to Pocotalego with Appleby's and Hewit[t]'s Companies, viz:

"Wise's[95] District is extended to Edisto, Robertson's[96] to Combahee, Buchanan Battery and one from Talliafero[97] dispensable. Wise should have two and Robertson four. What Batteries of the 6th should go to each district according to quality of guns and nature of country. Villepigue[98] Battery must go with Anderson between Combahee and Ashepoo."

Anderson is Colonel of the 5th Georgia Cavalry that passed here going to Adams Run a few weeks ago and I expect he is to relieve me. I am not sorry of being relieve[d] of the great responsibility I have here, but I prefer this place to Pocotalego.

Green Pond,
Dec. 5th, 1863

We got the worst whipping in the west that our army has had since the war began. Still if they have lost 40,000 men, it cannot be as bad as we thought and they are certainly not able to follow up their victory as they have retreated already. I am sorry to see by today's paper that Longstreet has had to give up the siege of Knoxville, but that he will take his command safely into Western Va.

# 1864

*Colonel Stokes finds himself posted where he did not want to go. Shortly after reporting to Pocotaligo, he requests a leave of twelve days to travel to the Upcountry "to acquire my negroes." (See Appendix I, No. 8.) While on leave, he sprains an ankle and requests a five-day extension. (See Appendix I, No. 9.) In addition to leave papers, see also a letter from Charleston concerning a sword, a separate response from the Confederate States General Purchasing Agent, and a General Order from the Department of South Carolina, Georgia, and Florida (See Appendix I, Nos. 10, 11, and 12). After his return, he again becomes involved with garrison duties such as drill and ceremonies.*

Pocotalego,
January 12, 1864

On my arrival at Coosawhatchie yesterday evening about 3 1/2 o'clock I found an order there for me to report to take command of the Regiment here during Col Rutledge's absence.

Pocotaligo,
Jan. 16th, 1864

Col R left here on Thursday on a fifteen days' leave and I do not care how soon he returns, for I prefer being in command of a post than here notwithstanding there is not half the work here that there is at a post. The Col has not got things here to suit me and as I am only temporarily in command, I do not care about making such changes as would suit me.

Pocotalego,
January 20, 1864

I am ordered to drill the Regiment before one of General W.'s Staff tomorrow morning for him to inspect the drill. I have not drilled any since I left Harderville[99] and must post myself.

Pocotaligo,
Jan. 27th, 1864

I went down to Port Royal Ferry to see the place and ride over the country between here & there. At the Ferry, I left my horse and walked down the causeway below where the pickets stand in the day to near the Bulk Head, saw the yankee pickets & when they saw me with two other men coming down the causeway they made some signal and I saw with my opera Glass all the guard double quicking[100] to them at the head of the causeway. I looked at them all good with my glass and saw all that I could see and then turned around and came back leaving them to wonder my business. The river is said to be about 300 yds across at that point. Still it does not look to be twice as wide as the Edisto, near enough for a good shot to kill a man with an Enfield rifle.[101] They did not show any desire to shoot me, though I do not know why the reason pickets came down so fast.

Pocotalego,
January 31st, 1864

I dined today at District Head Quarters, by invitation, with General Walker. They had a tolerably good dinner. We had a General Review yesterday and a good many ladies were out to see it. I had command of all the Artillery and Cavalry at the place. At the close of the Review Col Fort of the S. C. State Troops was publicly placed under arrest by General W. for publishing to his Regiment that if General W. did not muster them out of service that he would do so on Monday (as their term of service was out) and wrote a disrespectful letter to General W. to that effect. The General has taken him entirely away from his Regiment and sent him to report under arrest to Col Colcock at Grahamville.

Pocotalego,
February 3d, 1864

Our review was very good. General B.[eauregard] I understand was very much pleased with it. After it was over General W. sent one of his orderlies to ask me to come up to his

124

quarters and get an introduction to General B., which I did. He is a very pleasant man and has none of the "puff" about him. I spent about an hour up there with him when we all escorted him to the depot and saw him take the cars. He appears to be very sociable and fond of jokes.

Col R. has returned. He got back today. General W. seems to want me to remain here longer, but I will go up to see him about it tomorrow morning, but it will not be in time to write you in this. I am afraid they are trying to work me out of the place. Still I do not see how they can have the face to do so after offering me my choice.

The old State Troops were mustered out of service day before yesterday. Those under forty-five years were conscripted on the ground. A guard of about fifty men from the 32nd Georgia Volunteers (Col Harrison's) was placed around them and they are to be shipped direct from here to Columbia and from there they will be sent either to the west or Virginia. I think some of them are very uneasy. There will be about 125 or 150 conscripts in the Regiment. Col Fort is to be court martialed before he gets out.

*Colonel Stokes returns to Coosawhatchie with the premonition that it is only a matter of time before the 4th Regiment will join the fighting in Virginia.*

Coosawhatchie,
February 10th, 1864

You will see from the heading of this that I am at my Post at last and I could not desire to be more pleasantly situated than I am for the length of time that I have been here. I am occupying a nicely ceiled shed room about the size of ours with two glass windows which have just enough glass broken out to let in a sufficient quantity of air to suit my fancy, though they are out in the lower part of the window instead of the upper. I have a front room (large) for my office.

Coosawhatchie,
February 15, 1864

Appleby's Co. is ordered to Green Pond again and he marches with his Co. in the morning. Col Anderson's 5th Ga Cavalry that was there is here tonight on their way to Fla & Appleby's Co. is ordered there as one of the Companies to take his place. One whole Brigade of infantry from Charleston (Genl Colquit)[102] have passed here *en route* for Fla. Col Anderson just returned from Richmond the other day and I hear that he says the Sec[retary] of War told him that all of the Cavalry on the Coast would be sent out west and to Virginia, to take the places of those Regiments that are so much decimated under Stewart[103] and Wheeler[104] and send them to the coast to recruit. Another report is that Butler's[105] old Regt too is on their way to change with Colcock. I give you these reports as I get them. The former may be true, but the latter I doubt.

I am left here now with only five companies, about the same size command as that I had at Green Pond. Appleby's Co. hates awfully to go. They say they would not mind it so much if I was going with them.

It is very warm tonight and the wind is blowing a perfect March gale.

Coosawhatchie,
Feb. 17th, 1864

I am occupying the house that Maj Hauvey was in but not the same room. I am sleeping in the room that Genl R. E. Lee slept in when he had the house for his Hd. Qrs.

I hear the yanks are landing in force at St. Mary's, Fla. I think they are trying to draw as many of our troops off as possible by making something of a demonstration there and then attack us on this line somewhere. They are succeeding pretty well in drawing off a good many troops.

Feb. 18th, 1864

It is quite cold again. I see from a synopsis of the tax Bill just passed Congress that the confederate money is to be

126

heavily taxed so it will be a fine thing that the States will not take our corn.[106] You had better not sell more than enough corn etc. to have money on hand to meet the present demands, say four or five hundred dollars or less so that we may have very little on hand on the 1st of April.

Coosawhatchie,
Feb. 21st, 1864

. . . Another of my companies (Hewitt's) has been ordered to Green Pond and my artillery co. (Capt Tanabaux's) are under orders to be ready with 5 days' rations cooked to move at a moment's notice—it I think is to go to Fla. A good many more troops passed here in the last two days *en route* for Fla, and I understand the 11th Regt is to pass tonight. That demonstration of the Enemies in Fla is taking a lot of troops from this state. I have only Trenholm's Squadron & one infantry Company and the Section of artillery (2 guns) attached to Trenholm's Squadron under my command just now, if Tanabaux's Co. is moved. So you see my once large command is reduced to a skeleton.

I told you about Marshal getting very stiff from the hard ride down here. . . . I am very much afraid that without very light usage and rest that he will never get over it as he gets stiff after every ride of 15 or 20 miles I give him. As you see I am under the necessity of buying another horse. I have heard of three that are for sale, 2 of them at $1500— each and the other at $3000— The prices are tremendous, and I have not got the money to pay down for them and I will not think of giving that price unless the seller will take it in the present currency.

Get all the money you can in $5.— Bills that you will have on hand after the first day of April next, as $5.— Bills & under are not taxed.

Feb. 22nd. I got a letter from Capt Appleby. He is very much dissatisfied with his position and I believe all of his company. I expect they will be apt to appropriate me when they get with me again. I am sorry for them. I have a scheme on foot to get Barber here with me since my command has

127

been reduced & expect to go up and propose it to Genl W. tomorrow; do not know how I will succeed.

Coosawhatchie,<br>
Feb. 24th, 1864

I have but little to do now, my command is so much reduced, though Genl W. told me he thought it was only temporarily, but temporarily in the military sometimes turns out to be a long time. I have now Trenholm's two Cos. and the Co. of Artillery only & the latter is under marching orders. Hauvey's Batt is ordered to Savannah, Ga. and the Co. of his that I have is at the Depot waiting transportation. The train that takes them will soon be along, though Genl W– told me he had ordered a Co. to me from Hardeeville to take their place.

The reports you heard in regard to the Regt going west and what Rutledge said is false. He has more sense than to talk that way, that is, in saying he would not submit to the War Dept reducing the Regt. If they intend doing so, there is still a hope that it will not be done. Four Companies of Col Colcock's Regt have been under orders and are going to Ga. He has only three Companies under his command now, smaller then mine. I have been very creditably informed that the yanks only have a small garrison on Morris Island and it is thought that it can be retaken with two Regts & that Genl B– will likely try it. In fact it is said that information has been received at Dept Hd Qrs that the enemy's force is exceedingly small along the whole coast of S. C. I would not be surprised if we were sent West sometime this coming spring, though there are no orders to that effect as yet.

Thursday morning<br>
Feb. 25th, 1864

Hewitt & Appleby write that they want me very badly down there with them. I prefer remaining here now. The 11th Regt behaved very badly the other day in passing through in the cars. A great many jumped off and went home. All but six of Wescoat's Co. jumped off at Ashepoo.

Our victory is said to be complete in Fla. If so I suppose the troops will either return or go west. I look for Genl B–'s command to be very much drained in the next few months.

Coosawhatchie,<br>February 28th, 1864

I will not try my plan to get Barton's Company here. Since Colcock's Companies were ordered to Georgia it was useless to try. Lipscombe is Col of the 2nd S. C. C.[avalry] now. Gary is Colonel, I believe, of the 2nd S. C. I.[nfantry].

Coosawhatchie,<br>March 8th, 1864

I arrived here safe on Sunday about 12 1/2 o'clock.

Coosawhatchie,<br>March 10th, 1864

I am to be moved from here in May, so Col R– told me today. Genl W is to move his Hd Qrs to Grahamville in May and Col R is to be placed in command of the Post at Pocotaligo, and he told me today confidentially that he told Genl W– that he did not want to leave the Regt in command of Maj Emanuel and that he could not give the Post and the Regt both the attention they ought to have and that the Genl promised to order me to Pocotaligo to command the Regt. It is true it shows they both have confidence in me, but at the same time I do not like so much shifting about. It will put an end to my garden and all of my mess arrangements. I feel sure that Rutledge is the cause of it all, and that he particularly requested me to be sent back to command the Regt, though he did not tell me so. I am not to be ordered until Genl W– changes his Hd Qrs. Then you see it will be too late for a garden. I will have to send my sow & pigs home too then; they are doing finely. I think she is the most industrious sow I ever saw.

Coosawhatchie, S. C.
March 17th, 1864

I have heard no talk of our going to Va. recently, and it
would be impossible to reduce the troops on the coast any
more, just now, without replacing them with others & from a
dispatch that passed through the lines from Genl Beauregard in
Fla., it may be some time before the troops sent to Fla can
return. He said there were about 15000 troops of the enemy
in Jacksonville and a few more had arrived and that one Brigade
of the enemy were at Palatka;[107] that he would not be able to
return for some time yet.

I have just heard that Capt Mekler captured a yankee picket
boat last night, with four men in it, in Skull Creek near Hilton
Head Island.

*Although Colonel Stokes had not thought they were imminent, the
long-rumored orders for Virginia arrived. The next few weeks are
spent in preparation for the march and the campaign.*

Coosawhatchie, S. C.
Mar. 20th, 1864

I have just learned that the long talked of order, to go to Va.,
has come at last to Department Headquarters, and that our
regiment is to go. The operator at Charleston told the operator
here that four cavalry regiments[108] and Trenholm's Squadron
are ordered off, and that the 4th S. C. Cavalry is one. When
the orders to march will reach us, I do not know, but I suppose
in a few days; still I hope yet that Genl Butler may be able to
get it countermanded, for if it is not, the coast will be left in a
very destitute condition; it will only leave one cavalry regiment,
Kirk's Squadron, Patterson's Rangers, and two or three other
cavalry companies in the State of S. C. The order for these
regiments to move came from the Secretary of War, and Genl
Jordan,[109] who is in Charleston, telegraphed to Genl Butler,
who, you know, is in Florida, is how the operator in Charleston
heard it; so you see it must be pretty true.

130

March 21st . . . I have to [be at] a Board at Trenholm's Camp in a half hour.

I have just learned from a direct source that our Regt, the 5th, 6th & Trenholm's Squadron is certainly ordered & that the orders are to be extended this week.

Coosawhatchie, S. C.
Mar. 27th, 1864

I went up on the train Saturday and saw Col R. a few minutes, but learned little from him in regard to the movement of the Regt, except that he had received [an] order to have the Regt in light marching order. He does not know whether they will march through with all the men or send one man through to every three horses; though I rather think that every man will be required to march through on his horse, by the order extended from the War Department. I do not think the Regt will march in a body, but by squadrons, along different routes; or I rather think Col R. favors that mode; I do not.

I understand Capt A. and Hewett's companies are relieved from duty, and are ordered to report to their regiment, to move to the army of Northern Va. Capt A. was down to see Col R. yesterday after I left.

Coosawhatchie, S. C.
Mar 30th, 1864

The orders from the War Department have reached us, to move to the army of Northern Va. and report to Brig. Genl Butler; but with them came an order from Genl Butler's headquarters that we would not take up the march until a special order from his headquarters to that effect. It is thought we will very likely move some time next week.

Capt Trenholm has just returned from Columbia, where he saw Genl Hampton, who is charged in the order from the War Department with the prompt movement of the cavalry, and that he, (Genl H.) was to come down on Monday to see Genl Butler, and that the Regiment would be moved very soon; and that we all are to rendezvous in Columbia and get the horses shod. So I think there will be no doubt about our passing through Branchville.

I will not send my surplus things by express, as Capt McCurry[110] has promised to haul them as far as the nearest point we pass to my house.

I have applied to be relieved from the command of this post on the first day of April; Genl W. told me yesterday he would do it; and I also applied to Genl Gilmer[111] for a ten day's leave of absence.

Pocotaligo, S. C.
April 1st, 1864

I have been relieved from the command at Coosawhatchie and came to this place on yesterday evening.

I heard that Genl Hampton said we were to be in Columbia on the 10th; we are to stay there several days to have the horses shod, during which time we will have a big review. All of the cavalry order, viz: three regiments and five companies are to be there at the same time. That review will be worth seeing.

Col R. has just received a dispatch from Capt Pinckney,[112] who he sent to see Genl Hampton to know if he would allow him to send the Regt out by squadrons and by different routes; that the General consents to it. So the field officers will send their horses and servants with the second train, and will get about twenty days' furlough and then take the cars and meet the Regt at Petersburg, Va. So I do not know that I will take my ten day's leave, if it comes.

*Prior to departing for the assignment in Virginia, a Letter of Commendation from Captain William A. Courtenay in Hardeeville is forwarded to Colonel Stokes for his devotion to duty and gallant service on the coast.* (See Appendix I, No.13.)

Camp 4th S. C. Cavalry,
Near Columbia, S. C.
Apr 27th, 1864

I arrived here safely on time yesterday morning and, as I suppose you know, am anxious to hear something of the movements of the Regt, I will write you this evening.

The horses are not quite all shod yet; consequently the Regt will not move until Saturday next. The program has been somewhat changed, in accordance with instruction from the Secretary of War. All of the men who are on furlough are to join the Regiment at Greensboro, N. C., and are to march through on their horses. Inform R. Risher of the change.

Genl Hampton has turned over the movements of the troops from here, to Genl Butler, and Genl H. leaves for Richmond tonight. Col R. is to join us at Greensboro and go through with us also. So I suppose I will be relieved of the trouble of the command from there.

Genl W. S. Walker has been ordered to North Carolina, in command of Evans'[113] Brigade.

> Camp 4th S. C. Cavalry
> Camden, S. C.,
> May 1st, 1864

I left Columbia on Friday morning very hastily, to evade an order that was being issued to reduce the companies by taking of those who last joined and giving us back those dismounted men who were already transferred, which would have injured the Regt very much; so Genl Butler, Col R. and myself concluded it was best to get away at once. I arrived here Saturday evening about half past one o'clock, and am lying over here today, having what few horses that were unshod when we left Columbia, shod; and if they do not finish today, I may remain over again tomorrow. I hate very much to have work done on today, but we cannot help it.

*The preparations being completed, the 4th S. C. Cavalry, under Colonel Stokes' command, begins the march, in earnest, to Virginia.*

> Camp 4th S. C. Cavalry,
> On the march. Camden, S. C.,
> May 2nd, 1864

We got through shoeing all of the horses today.

133

Camp 4th S. C. Cavalry,
Enroute for Va.
Charlotte, N. C.,
May 6th, 1864

I have a great deal to tell you about our march and receptions at different points. I wrote you pretty fully from Camden, but Camden was nothing to what the good ladies of Lancaster District did for us.

At Lancaster C.[ourt] H.[ouse], I think there must have been from three hundred to five hundred ladies out to meet us; and a fine dinner on a long table, sufficient to have fed one thousand men, and I only had about three hundred fifty. We were welcomed to the dinner by Lieut Col Wiley, 5th S.C. Infantry, in a short but patriotic and very highly complimentary manner, which I replied to. Then our flag was crowned by Miss Stephens in a short and complimentary speech, to which my color sergeant replied, very happily. I then marched the command to the table, which was groaning with a variety of good things. When we were through, the men were told to fill their haversacks with the remainder; all was over by half past two o'clock.

We left the village yesterday morning, and about thirteen miles from there the ladies of N. C. and S. C., Lancaster District (it being on that line) had another fine dinner for us, where I stopped the Regt two hours to partake of. Pretty much the same ceremonies were gone through with as at the C. H., and the flag was again crowned by Miss Sureton, of N. C. I had again to reply to the speeches. We enjoyed the two hours extremely well. At this place an arch, made of cedar, was placed across the road for us to march under, with the following inscription: "We welcome our defenders."

At Pleasant Valley, still in Lancaster District, where we were to spend the night, a fine supper was awaiting us, which we partook of at half past six o'clock, but without the speaking, owing to the lateness of the day; more ladies and another pleasant time.

But alas! We are now out of the old Palmetto State, and we meet no more receptions.

The ladies, accompanied by the officers and soldiers, at each place, went all through our camp. I do think, without exception, that the people of Lancaster District are the most hospitable I ever saw. The ladies showered us with flowers on every occasion.

> Camp 4th S. C. Cavalry,
> On march,
> Salisbury, N. C.,
> May 8th, 1864

I arrived a few minutes ago, (three o'clock P. M.). We marched twenty-two miles today; and it hardly seemed like Sunday, only as we would meet people going to church.

> Camp 4th S. C. Cavalry,
> Greensboro, N. C.,
> May 12th/64

I arrived here on yesterday evening, all safe and sound, Col R. and the furloughed portion of the command awaiting me. We will be over here until tomorrow, to get some horses shod. We got [an] order here to keep on as fast as possible. The Col will accompany us from here; so I will be relieved of the trouble of the command of the Regiment.

I had to ford the Yadkin six miles this side of Salisbury, and anticipated some trouble, but got over the command safely. The river was about three hundred yards wide and caught the horses about half saddle skirt. Col Dunovant's[114] Regiment preceded us.

*In the previous letter, Colonel Stokes enclosed a clipping from the* Charlotte Daily Times, *May 7, 1864:*

ARRIVAL OF CAVALRY. Yesterday afternoon, about one o'clock, the fine Regiment of Cavalry, under command of Lieut. Col. Stokes, and known as the 4th South Carolina, arrived in Charlotte enroute for duty at the point assigned them.

135

The men are fine specimens of the army, and they were well mounted and equipped. The display made by the Regiment, while passing through the heart of the city, was highly gratifying. We are sure they will do good service when they confront the enemy.

*The 4th Regiment has now reached Virginia. The next several letters describe action associated with Grant's attempt to take Richmond. Colonel Stokes' command made up part of Lee's plan to defend against the approaches to the Confederate capital. The fighting is fierce, and includes the Battle of Hawes' Shop, an important crossroads about ten miles east of Mechanicsville on the way to Richmond.*

Camp 4th S. C. Cavalry,
Clarksville, Va.,
May 18th/64

I will write you a short letter from this place, as you may be somewhat uneasy from what I wrote you about the enemy's raiding party in our road.

We received a dispatch at Oak Hill night before last from the A. Q. M., A. C. S. [Assistant Quartermaster, Army of the Confederate States], and the ordnance officers of this place, that the enemy were within thirty miles and moving on it, and asking us to hasten on to its defence. We armed about two hundred fifty men with all the sabres and pistols we had and sent them on, but on arriving here we learned that the raiding party was bearing down on the Peninsula to Butler's army.[115] We have sent off to reconnoitre the country ahead of us, before moving this morning, and hope we will not meet them until our Regiment has gotten their arms again.

We crossed the Roanoke this morning, and then there will be no river between us and the enemy, if they have not gone back; and a gentleman has just reported to us that he heard that they were within twelve miles yesterday of Christianville. We go to Christianville tonight, if the way is open. We mean to use every precaution we can to avoid them until the Regiment is armed.

The upper portion of N. C. we found all right, but the

difference was very perceptible as soon as we crossed the Virginia line. Virginia seems to be as strong as S. C. This place is very enthusiastic in our cause. The ladies shower us with boquets and bow to every soldier as they pass, and the people along the road meet us with warm bread and buttermilk and butter, also tobacco.

Camp 4th S. C. Cavalry,
Kingsville, Va.,
May 19th/64

We did not go to Christianville as I wrote you from Clarksville we would, as Col R. got some alarming reports of the enemy's raiding party being there, which proved to be false.

As soon as a little over half of the Regiment had got across the Roanoke River, which we had to cross in flats,[116] (7)[117] (the river was about four hundred [yards] wide), he immediately moved off with them for Roanoke station, fifteen miles out of the way, and sent me word to come on as fast as possible with the others, as soon as they got over, which took two hours. So we had to make a forced march to overtake him, which we did about 5 P. M. He sent me no instruction, and I did not know what caused him to change his route until I got up; he also ordered the wagons to be left. So you can imagine what sort of a night I spent, with nothing but my indian-rubber overcoat and only about half shingle; he and D. G. were pretty much in my fix.

We were given something on the road to eat yesterday, but did not get our breakfast this morning until twelve M., which we paid $3.33 for.

The wagons will be up with us tonight again, and I hope the Col will not take such another wild goose chase.

Camp 4th S. C. Cavalry
In 10 miles Richmond, Va.,
May 23/64

I am now in ten miles of Richmond, where we spent the night, with but little for man or horse, and expect to be in the city by eleven or twelve o'clock today.

137

May 24th: We passed through the city about twelve M., and are encamped four miles on the other side of the city, on the Brooks' Turnpike Road. There was no demonstration on our passing through, as I suppose it was nothing uncommon; several persons asked what brigade it was. We are to remain here for two days and then go to the front, either to Lee or Beauregard; I have not learned whom yet.

Genl Lee is at Hanover C.[ourt] H.[ouse],[118] some twenty miles, and Genl B. is near Drewey Bluff; and the report is that Grant is changing his base to the peninsula. If so, I suppose the whole army will be concentrated there.

We are encamped near where Stewart[119] was killed in a battle with that raiding party about one month ago.

Our horses are not getting more than one-third food, and we are on the shortest sort of rations ourselves; it has begun to tell on the horses. Marshal's[120] back has become a little sore within the last three or four days.

I took dinner at the Exchange Hotel, kept by George McMaster, for S. C. officers and soldiers.

Camp 4th S. C. Cavalry,
Near Richmond, Va.,
May 25th/64

I saw Genl [M. C.] Butler yesterday, and he told me that we were to go to the front tomorrow, (Thursday) and that he was going with us; that we are to go to Lee's army near Hanover Junction, about twenty miles from here, and I think the probabilities are very great that the Regiment may be placed into action very soon, as the yankee army is pressing on Lee very hard. In fact, Richmond is very closely besieged on the north and east, defended by Lee and Beauregard, two able Generals; and notwithstanding they may be pressed hard, still I think we will come out all right in the end.

You will doubtless be surprised to hear that the raiding party that killed Stuart, got within two miles of Richmond, up to our last lines of breastworks, and could have taken them had they known how small our garrison was.

Head Quarters
Fourth S. C. Cavalry,
On North Side
South Anna, Va.
May 27th, 1864

We are now just below (some two miles) the Hanover
Junction encamped on the North Anna, within a short distance
of General Lee's Head Quarters awaiting orders from General
Hampton, whose Head Quarters are about five miles from us.

Grant is evidently changing his base to the Peninsula to
make a junction with Butler,[121] "the Beast," and the signs are
evident that General Lee is moving his army to confront them.
The sick, ambulances, Artillery, etc. are passing here now,
9:30 A.M., and I expect we will move tonight somewhere.
I do not know where it will be, but think the main body will
move back on Richmond. Heavy skirmishing has been going
on all the morning and we hear the rifles distinctly. We are
near the 6th S. C. Infantry.

We are now in the midst of Lee's Army and it is certainly
interesting, to us, who have been on the coast. The wagon
trains alone occupy miles. The troops are in the best possible
spirits and are wishing for Grant to attack us here, but he knows
our lines are too strong for him and he prefers changing the
seat of war to the Peninsula. Both armies are between the
North and South Anna and are only divided by an imaginary
line and General Lee could give them the "deuce", but he
prefers not to make an attack and rather follow Grant to the
Peninsula than to do so, so I have heard.

This is certainly the Army of the Confederacy.

Since Stuart has been killed I hear there will be no more
Cavalry Corps, but that each of the Major Generals will have
a division and report direct to General Lee.

Camp of Fourth S. C. Cavalry
near Atlett[122] Station, Va.
Central R.R.
11 miles north of Richmond,
May 29th, 1864

(Battle of Hawes' Shop)

Yesterday about four miles from here, near the Pamunky[123] River, we had for about three or four hours a very severe engagement with the advance army of Grant, and by the blessing of God alone I am safe, also Capt Appleby and R. Risher.

General Hampton fought a Yankee Cavalry Corps and two Corps of infantry[124] with only his Cavalry Division, about 7,000 strong, so you can see the odds which we fought against. General Butler was not with us and Col R. was in command of the Brigade, so he was not with us and I was in command of the Regiment and the only Field Officer present, Maj E. being left at Richmond. Our Regiment has suffered very seriously and fought most gallantly until the enemy turned our left flank, that was defended by the Third Virginia Cavalry, and we were ordered to fall back, which we did firing on the enemy. I held my line in perfect order until we were nearly surrounded and were ordered to fall back. We were beaten from our position by overwhelming forces but not routed. I was ordered by General Fitz Hugh Lee[125] to charge the enemy with my loaded guns and deliver my fire when near and to go in with a shout which we did and delivered the fire when within about fifty yards and then sheltered my men behind the trees as much as possible. Where we fought was tolerably thick undergrowth and a good many trees about twelve inches in diameter, which we took shelter behind, but we had to fall back through an open field and a number of the men were lost there. I had in action about three hundred exclusive of horse holders and as far as we can ascertain there are about 125 killed, wounded and missing and among them some of our most valuable and gallant officers and men. General Hampton met me as I was falling back and told me that I did all he expected me to do and to get my men to their horses as soon as I could and fall behind the second line of defence. Col R. was generous enough to tell General Hampton and Brig Gen Butler that I deserved the credit for the fight our Regiment made.

A Va. soldier told me that it was the hottest fight they had ever been in. We were under fire for three hours, but were only actively engaged for about one half hour, and you see our loss in that little time.

Skirmishing is going on now with the men and our Infantry. We expect a big battle to come off near here as the enemy are on this side of the Pamunky trying to make down to the Peninsula.

A list of the casualties will be published.

Killed, Wounded and Missing at Battle of Hawes' Shop.

Killed—Capt Price and in hands of the enemy.
Wounded seriously in left arm—Capt D. S. Smily.
Wounded in right arm and missing—Sergeant P. W. Fairey.
Wounded and missing—S. S. Canady.
Wounded—Private J. C. Utsey—seriously in right leg.
Wounded—Private John Goodwin—in right side seriously.
Wounded—Private John Kinsey—in right shoulder seriously.
Missing—Privates John Smily, L. Kinard, J. D. McAlhany and Daniel Smoke.

The above is the list of casualties in Capt Appleby's Company.

*Next, Colonel Stokes describes the fighting around Cold Harbor, Gaines' Mill, Mechanicsville, and the Chickahominy, as Grant continued to hammer at Lee's defensive line protecting Richmond.*

Camp Fourth S. C. Cavalry,
Gains Mill,
June 2nd, 1864

Yesterday evening the enemy made a sharp attack on us about 6:30 o'clock about two miles in front and we were ordered up, but it was all over by the time we got there. We were in another sharp battle again on Monday the 30th with

141

our Cavalry Brigade under Butler and I was placed in command on the right wing of the skirmishers by General Butler which placed me under a sharp fire for about an hour and a half or two hours, but I am thankful to say that I came out through the goodness of God safe, though more exhausted than I think I ever was in my life before. When the fight was about half through I found a horse in the woods where I was fighting and mounted him and rode through the remainder of the fight or I certainly could not have held out. I was placed in command of a Geo. Batt. and they gave me trouble to keep them up to the mark. Lieut McCrorey is reported to be killed and in the hands of the enemy. Our engagement on the 30th was like that of the day before against a heavy force of the enemy Infantry and Cavalry and we had to fall back. The men fought well until their ammunition gave out before we were ordered to fall back and then the head of the horse holders got into a stampede and a good many of them ran off shamefully, and I am sorry to say that there were some from our Regiment as well as from all of the other portion of the command engaged. In the fight of the 30th the Regiment lost fifty-four killed, wounded and missing. We have lost seriously in officers. The Drags.[126] and Barber's[127] Company have but one officer but what is killed, wounded or missing and the other companies are nearly as bad. We have a large force here now and the enemy are skirmishing heavily on our left. Butler, "the Beast," is said to be moving his force here and General Beauregard is moving his round to confront him. Some of General Beauregard's force came by here yesterday and last night. Some portions of our force have been in action every day since Saturday and it is dreadfully cut up and we are all completely worn out. I never was so worn out in all my life and have a very bad cold and cough. Have had but little rest since I left Richmond.

Capt A., Lieut Gen Williams[128] and R. Risher's Company safe. His Company lost seven wounded and three were the two Wells and P. Thomas.

On the March near
Bottom Bridge on the
Chickahominy River,
June 2nd, 1864

We are now on the Peninsula confronting the right wing of Grant's army again and may have to feel it again, as our Generals call those two last engagements I wrote you we were in, but I hope not for our Regiment is badly cut up and we all need rest before we should be put into action again. We have been marching, fighting or in line ever since we left Richmond eight days ago, not even time enough to change our clothes, and sometimes forty-eight hours without anything for man or beast, with the earth for our bed and the canopy of heaven for our cover.

All are cheerful and the greatest regret is that we have lost so many valuable lives.

The fight was a very unfortunate one and nothing was gained by continuing it so long. I suppose there will be no rest for the Cavalry until the great battle[129] is over, for they have to feel and locate the enemy and our Generals feel too long sometimes. General Butler is not popular with the Brigade. He wants to be too stiff, though he seems to find a good many things for me to do for him and gives me pretty hot places in action.

Lieut Bell is missing and supposed to have been killed in the stampede the night after the battle by the 21st Ga. Batt.

Camp Fourth S. C. Cavalry
near Savage Station,
York River R.R.
Near Botton Bridge,
June 4th, 1864

We have gone into camp again this evening and brought up the wagon train and servants, which have been a few miles to the rear for the past five days, and I hope we will be permitted to enjoy the Sabbath (tomorrow) in quietude. A heavy battle was raging all day yesterday to our left, near that once noted battleground, (Gains Mill)[130] until about 9 o'clock P. M. The

143

enemy made a number of assaults during the day and two after dark, when they were made well nigh drunk, each of which was repulsed with the greatest sort of slaughter on the part of the enemy, our loss being comparatively small. During three assaults I was not very far from the battle field and the roar of musketry was terrific in the extreme, and having recently passed through such trying ordeals, I deeply sympathize with our brave soldiers in the trenches. The ground in front of our trenches are said never to have been so thickly strewn with dead Yankees.[131] We have not tried to dislodge them; therefore each side holds their position, or I should have tried to have visited the battle field.

Skirmishing is still going on daily between the pickets and the army in line of battle and I have heard a number since I commenced this. Our camp is only about 2 1/2 miles from our advance line. During Saturday's fight, the 28th, a party of the enemy charged up to the line of the Regiment near where I had my position, and within about twenty yards of me, and shouted out "surrender" several times; whereupon I ordered the men to fire on them which they did, and made several of them bite the dust and the others gave back and I drew off the men firing on them. It happened just as I was ordering the men to fall back.

This is the portion of the country occupied, you know, by McClellan[132] and through which he made his hasty retreat: visible signs of the retreat can still be seen in the way of old clothes, haversacks, etc.

Late in the evening Saturday.

I am just ordered off. I go to the front.

Sunday morning,
June 5th, 1864

The command was not kept out long last night before it returned. It was a dreadful rainy night.

Bivouac on
White Oak Swamp,
14 Miles below Richmond,
June 7th, 1864

On Sunday evening we were ordered to this place and are sending out two squadrons at a time on picket duty. How much longer we will remain here I cannot say, but the way we have been moving it is time we were on the go again. We are here in the advance and our wagon train, servants, etc. are still at Savage Station, where our rations are cooked up and sent to us. The ration we draw is a plenty, if we could get something for our servants and could have time to cook it after we draw it. The bulk of the ration is 1/2 pound bacon, one and 1/8 pound flour or meal, a few peas and sugar and coffee can be gotten by droping 1/8 of the bacon. Our moving about so much is owing entirely to the movements of the enemy. We must confront him wherever he goes. My opinion is that Grant is virtually whipped now and that we will not have the big battle that is so generally looked for, but that we may have a succession of smaller ones, such as that fought on Wednesday and Friday.

We are now on one of the great battle fields of McClellan's retreat and the bones of two dead Yankees that were never found to be buried are lying near here. We have only about half of the Regiment here. The other half are in hospital and at the wagon camp sick or with sore back horses. General B. had been very much blamed in the Brigade, for his action in Monday's fight, the 30th.

P. S. Grant has been remarkably quiet the past two days and reports have it that he is moving on down in this direction which gets him further from Richmond. I think he is at a loss to know what to do. Malvern Hill is only six miles from here.

Mechanicsville, Virginia,
June 8th, 1864

We have left the Peninsula and are here again and we are to leave for somewhere with Genl H. tomorrow morning.

I think Genl H. is going after Sheridan, who is said to be on the Pamunky committing depredation. Skirmishing is still going on along our line and all wish for the final battle to come.

*On June 7, Grant sent two divisions of cavalry under the command of Brigadier General Philip H. Sheridan on a mission against the Virginia Central Railroad. He also instructed General Hunter to join forces with Sheridan and for them to join the Army of the Potomac. Sheridan was met by General Hampton at Trevilian's Station on June 12. In Hampton's Cavalry was Colonel Stokes and the 4th. In a hotly contested battle, Sheridan was forced to retreat without accomplishing his mission. The following letters tell of this battle and of ensuing engagements during the beginnings of the siege of Petersburg.*

Near Louisa Court House<br>June 14th, 1864

We met Sheridan with his three Divisions on last Saturday near Newark on the Central R.R. in Louisa County and fought him the whole day until night closed the fight, capturing a great number of prisoners and we lost a good many, who were surrounded and went into the enemy's lines [mistaking them] for ours. I ran my horse up in about one hundred yards of the enemy's battery [mistaking it] for one of ours, not knowing the ground [becoming disoriented], and made a narrow escape in getting off. At another time during the day General B. and myself who were protecting the rear were cut off and had to charge through to make our escape. The fight was again renewed on Sunday evening and lasted about four hours, when we repulsed them at every point and completely routed them about dark, but were not able to follow them up owing to the darkness of the night. They are now on the North Side of the North Anna and we are still pursuing them. Through the mercy of God I am still safe, also Appleby and W. B. and R. Risher.

Maj E. and Adjutant Manigault are prisoners. The Regt lost about one hundred, killed, wounded and missing in the two

146

engagements, mostly captured. Col Aiken was seriously wounded. Col Dunovant was wounded on the 28th of May. Col R. is unwell and I am second in command in the Brigade.

Warleys Tavern,
North Side North Anna,
June 15th, 1864

Sheridan has changed his course towards Fredericksburg and we are going north after him again.

Capt A. lost no men on the last two fights. One or two were wounded and captured, but recaptured again.

Col R. is sick and was sent back to the reserve camp near Richmond and I have out about 170 of the men of the Regiment with me whose horses are fit for duty. I. M. Liston[133] got his horse killed in Saturday's (last) fight. We are all completely worn out by hard fighting and forced marches both day and night, but all are in fine spirits and willing to keep on.

Our rations gave out and we were forty-eight hours without any.

We were in nine miles of the Blue Ridge and could see them distinctly. In Saturday's fight portions of our Regiment made several charges on horse-back and each time the yanks gave way. Portions of our ordnance train was captured Saturday, but we charged the enemy and retook it. Persons who participated in the noted Brandy Station[134] fight say this [was] a sharper engagement. Sunday's fight was dismounted altogether on our part and the enemy charged us no less than four times dismounted and on horseback and was each time repulsed with great slaughter. Their loss on that day is supposed to be some 500 killed, wounded and missing, while our side was not more than fifty. Our Regiment only lost one killed and about two wounded. Our Brigade was the principal troop engaged that day supported by a Virginia Brigade. The yankee dead are strewn in every direction and a great number of their wounded are left in a hospital near by with a Surgeon and Asst. Surgeon. My escape on Sunday was very narrow indeed. A cannon ball struck some rails about twelve feet from me and passed only a few inches over my back. Had the rails not been there it would have cut me in two. We captured a good many horses, arms and equipments.

We will have active times for some days yet I think.

Near Matapony River,<br>
East of Fredericksburg R.R.,<br>
June 17th, 1864

We are away off here still, in pursuit of the enemy, who are only a few miles on the north side of the river moving down, I think, to join Grant and I think General H. is trying to prevent it.

All this country has recently been occupied by the enemy and the people are certainly in a destitute and distressing condition. They seem so glad to see a Confederate again.

The command is ready to move.

Wickham Station, Virginia<br>
Central R.R. on<br>
Pomonky River,<br>
South Side, June 19th, 1864

I am now in about twenty miles of Richmond and as I thought was on my way back from this long and tedious trip after Sheridan, but received an order last night to be ready to march at 4 o'clock A. M. prepared for action. And I learned that we are to go to the old church[135] where we fought on the 30th of May, I suppose to intercept Sheridan should he come that way. I wrote you of the two last fights we had above Louisa Court House on the 11th and 12th, at Trevillian, when we whipped him, killing and wounding about 600 and took about 500 prisoners and pursued him around by Bowling Green and down the south side of the Matapony, he going down the north side, and forced him, as I understood yesterday, before we left to cross his command below the junction of the two rivers, where they had to be boated over. He killed his horses, which became broken down, to prevent us from getting them, at the rate of about fifteen horses to every mile, so scouts report. We passed down a portion of the road that he retreated on, and I never saw the like of dead horses in my life.

General Butler is in command of the Division and placed me yesterday in command of the Brigade. I am acting Brigadier General.

Bottom Bridge,
June 22nd/64

I received four letters from you yesterday while lying in line of battle around the White House about one mile from it and while the shells were frequently exploding over me. . . . We are now within 4 miles of White Oak swamp where we started from. Bottom Bridge is one mile below where the York R.R. crosses the Chickahominy River. You can see what a circuit we made by Louisa C.[ourt] H.[ouse]; thence near by Bowling Green, then back across [the] Pamunkey River and down to the White House on the York River and across here. Where we will go from here I have no idea but think we will remain near here for several days to prevent Sheridan from joining Grant. He crossed at the White House night before last. We dashed on the pickets at the White House on Sunday morning and captured 17 and had the whole command been up Genl H– could have dashed on the place and taken it, I think with little loss & captured a large wagon train of some one or two hundred in number; but the ememy had some of their gun boats to protect the place and two fired off in truth nearly with about 2.000 cav. & infantrymen skirmished with them, both Monday and Tuesday until we found out that Sheridan had crossed and then we drew off & came here last night and the Regt did not lose anyone. I passed near where we fought through the 28th to 30th of May and got a list of all of our wounded that fell into the hands of the enemy from a lady at whose house they had their Hospital and saw the graves of the wounded that died. Among them was Sam Canaday.

Reserve Camp
Near Richmond,
June 23rd, 1864

I came up here last night and am going to return to the Regiment this morning.

The Reserve Camp has been removed to the South side of the James River near the Coal Pits.

I left the Cavalry front about 3 P. M. yesterday. All was quiet. There is no telling where I will find them on my return. A great number of our horses are used up and if we do not get some rest soon the whole Regiment will be used up.

Col R. returned to camp yesterday was how I got off this long.

Ladds Store,
Charles City Co.,
June 25th, 1864

We attacked the enemy's cavalry at this point yesterday evening about 4 o'clock and after about two hours hard fighting drove them from every position in confusion, with but little loss to ourselves, taking one or two pieces of Artillery and capturing some of the wagons and a number of prisoners, among them one colonel. We formed in a regular line of battle, dismounted and charged and drove them from every position, our Regiment leading the charge. A captain that we captured said, "I hear that they use to not saddle their horses for the Virginia Cavalry, but since Butler's Brigade got here they had to learn." The Virginia Cavalry or some of them I know move very soon. Our Brigade stands high as fighters both with the enemy and our troops. Our Enfield Rifles are the things to do the work. We have captured nearly enough carbines, sharps, etc. to arm our Regiment, but I prefer the Enfield. As soon as we drive the enemy from the field the Virginia troops run in and plunder it, consequently our boys get very little. I passed a very fine saddle on a dead horse, that I wanted, but did not have time to get it and when we turned back from the pursuit everything was gone. A bridle and halter is all that I have gotten yet. I continued the pursuit some two or three miles where I finally broke down as did most of the Regiment [the horses were exhausted] and the mounted Cavalry came up so we stopped for our horses and last night returned and slept on the battle field.

We lost only two killed in the Regiment and five or six wounded, none killed or wounded in Capt A.'s Company. Our boys have learned how to protect themselves, though we only had a little over a hundred in the fight.

We lay in line of battle all day before the fight began.

Near Drewry's Bluff,
June 26th., 1864

I could not leave the Regiment, being in command, Col R. being in command of the Brigade.

The news is that Grant is recrossing the James again is why we are awaiting orders, so I have no idea where we will go, but am very sure we will go somewhere tomorrow morning, but we ought not to go anywhere if it could be avoided for the next three or four days at least, for we are perfectly worn out both man and horse. The officers and men of the Regiment (they tell me) are perfectly surprised at what I have gone through with and I have been told by a number of the Regiment that my action in battle has been spoken of in the highest terms from the Col on down and that I have the entire confidence of the Regiment. My reply is that I usually try to do my duty and am glad to see that my efforts are appreciated.

Stoney Creek Station,
R. & W. R. R.
June 28th, 1864

We are twenty miles from Petersburgh on the Weldon Railroad waiting for Kaut's[136] and Wilson's[137] raiders, who are expected to rejoin Grant by this route and some say they are expected here this evening. We put it on to Sheridan just right and I feel sure that we will whip them if they come, though so many of our horses have given out and been sent to the reserve

151

camp that our force is very small in numbers, but strong in heart. We fought Sheridan two days at Trevillian Station, whipped him and chased him to retreat in great confusion and skirmished two days at the White house, which resulted favorably to us. On Friday, 25th, we fought him again at Nance's Shop[138] below Bottom Bridge and whipped him and drove him some six miles, until 9 o'clock P. M. Now we are over here, so you can imagine what some of us (for there are but few of us here that have gone through it all) have gone through with in the last twenty days. We stayed one night on this side of the James. I passed through Petersburgh yesterday about two P.M.

I think we will be over here for some time unless Grant concludes to change his base again. Both armies are confronting each other near and to the east of Petersburgh with Grant's left resting not far from here. Grant is near enough to carry out Gilmore's[139] disgraceful plan at Charleston of shelling the helpless inhabitants of the place. When the big fight will come off I can not say or whether it will come at all. I want to see it over; then we may get some rest which is much needed.

*Believing that Colonel Stokes was still away at the reserve camp, William Appleby, not knowing of the colonel's return to duty, writes his aunt (Mrs. Stokes) on June 30, 1864. (See Appendix I, No. 14.) Meanwhile, additional combat action is related in a letter dated the same day as Appleby's letter.*

Stoney Creek Station,
Petersburgh & Weldon R.R.
June 30th, 1864

Wilson's raiders were expected here the evening I wrote you. They came down that evening and attacked us about three miles from here (below) five times during the night and we repulsed them each time and just at daylight we got in their rear and attacked them and they broke and ran at once. We captured a number (over 100) horses and men and pursued them for several miles, when we were withdrawn to cut them off at another point. In their flight they threw away some 50,000 cartridges and a number of other things, but unfortunately our

Brigade got but little of the plunder. I got a nice pair of scissors (small), this paper and a pocket comb. I was on foot and about the time I gave out I met one of my couriers with a captured horse and mounted him. Yesterday evening we met them some seven miles above here and after one volley at them some four hundred surrendered. We have been capturing them in every direction and I have just heard that one man captured some 75 prisoners, so you may judge how we had them routed. I think we will capture about 2/3 or 3/4 of his force and I wish they were nearly all dead for they have done us a good deal of damage. In their camp yesterday we found all kinds of ladies' apparel that the rascals had stolen on their raid. They had their own way until we got after them; a few of them have succeeded I think in getting to Grant's army already, through by-roads and I expect he will try to relieve him, if they are not all captured before his assistance comes. We are all completely worn out and our horses. Have only fifty men able in the Regiment to go after them, but they go cheerfully. The most of our Regiment are at the reserve [camp] or gone to Richmond to get their horses shod, so we haven't a command for a captain. I have just heard that all the wagon train (some 80) and Artillery were captured by General Lee's Cavalry Division who got after them as soon as we routed them.

*Apparently having been wounded, Colonel Stokes next writes from a hospital. When he is released, he does not return immediately to combat but is given duty with a Board of Officers.* (See Appendix I, Nos. 15 and 16.)

Hugenot Springs Hospital,
July 7th, 1864

Capt Busbee, Colcock, and Mr. Banks are here and all are improving. I am in a room with two Virginia Lieutenants of Cavalry, very nice men. Another Lieutenant has been added to the room this evening. There are about 500 patients here.

I have heard from the Brigade since I left. They have been doing nothing, but lying up recruiting,[140] which they certainly needed very much, and I hope they will not have anything to

153

do in the next two or three weeks.

Before I left the command the other day we had only 55 men present in the Regiment. Some 75 had been sent to Richmond to have their horses shod and all the others were at the reserve camp so you see Col R. and myself had a small command, two field officers to 55 men. And Genl B– had only about 150 men in his whole Brigade. The Cavalry has never had such an active campaign as this has been.

Hugenot Springs Hospital,<br>
July 10th, 1864

I will leave here tomorrow morning (Monday) for the front. Dr Walker has about 650 patients in the hospital now.

I suppose you see how frightened the yanks are about the reported force at Harper's Ferry and other points north of that. It is General Early[141] with twenty-odd thousand Infantry and 4000 Cavalry. I think General Lee has sent them to draw Grant off from Petersburgh and change the seat of war north, and to get the large amount of supplies that there are in the valley, which are being brought in daily. We are in the midst of a dreadful drought here, no rain for about six weeks.

Stoney Creek Station, 4 P.M.<br>
July 13th, 1864

I have just arrived here and have learned that the Regiment is still 10 miles from here.

General B. has Col Rutledge under arrest, but do not know the particulars.

Malone's Farm near<br>
Reams Station, P.& W. R.R.,<br>
July 14th, 1864

We are about ten miles from Stoney Creek Station now, about three or four miles south of the R.R. I arrived here safely yesterday evening about sunset and found all quiet. Col R. had just received a note from Genl B. releasing him from arrest. His arrest I think a rather extraordinary affair. It seemed that some of the men of the 6th Regiment and some of ours had gone into some man's oats field and brought in some oats for their horses without permission and Maj Morgan of the 5th Regiment saw them and wrote a note to Genl B. that he had seen men of the 4th and 6th Regiments bringing in oats and asked if his men might get some. The General sent this note to Col R. and asked if he gave these men permission and he said he had not and that he wished the General would punish them severely, whereupon the General sent down and ordered him under arrest. The Officers generally think it very unjust and the General must have thought so himself by releasing him so soon. The Col is very much mortified at it. I was appointed the Pres. of a Board to examine officers about one month ago and the board has never had an opportunity to assemble and as we are quiet now the General wants us to assemble tomorrow, which we will do if nothing prevents. I dislike being on such a board, but as I have been placed there without my knowledge or consent I shall try to do my duty fearlessly and impartially. I am afraid that our quiet will not last long as the enemy's Cavalry are reported in motion again. Still it is so warm and our horses have recruited so little that I would much prefer their remaining quiet for a month yet. Still if they will come on we will give them the best we have, which I rather think they will find quite enough.

> Malone's Farm near
> Reams Station, P.&W.
> July 17, 1864

The news from Early is very encouraging. I hope he may be able to take Washington and Baltimore both. I hear that Burnside[142] with his corps has gone to Charleston. If so a desperate effort will be made to take the place. Grant, finding himself unable to accomplish his object[ive] here, is making diversions in other directions to cover his defeat.

The opinion is that Sheridan will try to cut the Central R.R. again soon. If so we will soon be on the north side of the James. Our horses are in bad condition to meet a set of raiders on fresh horses. Still I think we can manage them.

Malone's Farm near
Reams Station, P.& W.R.R.
July 19, 1864

I am comfortably quartered in a room of Maj Malone's house, which he kindly permitted us to use for the assembly of the examining board, which I have been sitting on since last Friday. This is about a quarter of a mile from the camp.

We have an old tent stretched in camp, but it leaks badly; still it is some protection and we should be thankful. We are getting on very well in the way of rations, both for man and horse and if we could only be quiet here for a month, the horses would improve very much. General H., I understand, says this campaign has been the most active by far of any previous one in this state and I think he might have added that the victories of the Confederates have been more decisive. An officer told me a day or two ago that he had made an estimate of Sheridan and Wilson's loss in all the engagements since we have been here and that it was from ten to thirteen thousand in killed, wounded and missing. Wilson's raiders against the Danville R.R. are said to have been between six and seven thousand and I understand that we have sent off thirty-six hundred (3600) prisoners besides the killed, so you see they could not have gotten back with many. Our Brigade has contributed not a little to these favorable results and its merits and fighting qualities are being acknowledged very generally, but the troops that have been here all the time are jealous of us.

The news from General Early is conflicting, but there is no doubt he has gotten a large amount of supplies and secured the whole Yankee ration. The latest report is that he has recrossed the Potomac. Grant and General Lee's armies are still confronting each other before or around Petersburg, with our Cavalry on the right flank of General Lee's line. We may remain here several days or weeks yet, but I am afraid not.

The Board has just gotten through with its session for today and it is still raining.

156

Camp 4th S. C. Cavalry,
Malone's Farm
July 20th, 1864

It is still cloudy & bids fair to rain again. We spent the
night very comfortably under our old tent (the Col, Dr G. &
myself). . . . I will keep my eyes open for the yanks, but I have
seen so much of the Blue coat rascals that I am tired of seeing
them. I hear that something in regard to a charge that Calhoun
made with his squadron mounted at Trevilian Station was published in the Charleston papers; if you have seen it cut it out
and send it to me. I want to see it. It was not considered so
brilliant & we are surprised that it should be written in the
paper & the action of no one else noticed. Anything you see in
the State's papers in regard to the Regt, be sure to cut it out
and send it to me. This young Captain has unfortunately given
out or was suddenly stricken sick in two fights and there is a
good deal of talk about it in the Regt.

Camp 4th. S. C. Cavalry,
Malone's Farm,
July 22nd., 1864

I am here still, but no one has any idea how much longer we
will remain. I had no idea we would have been here this long.
We are all lying quiet here now. Grant has contracted his
lines a little, but both armies are about as strongly entrenched
as they can be. Shelling is kept up daily from both sides
without any material effect. The report is that Grant has been
killed, but no one believes it; still it may be so. I am uneasy
about our army in the West, am afraid Atlanta will fall.
Johnson[143] has been relieved of the command, but I do not
know for what. Still I suppose it was on account of his retreating so much.
Capt A. is on picket now. He has behaved very well in all the
engagements out here and has been through them all. His
company has behaved well. R. Risher is considered one of the
best orderlies in the Regiment. Capt Barber is still sick at the
Hugenot Spring[s] Hospital. He was with us in only two

157

fights, but behaved remarkably well. I. M. Liston's horse was not killed as he told me he was and he has him again.

Camp 4th S. C. Cav.
Malone's Farm,
July 28th, 1864

You will no doubt have seen the result of the invasion into M'd. before this time.

A report just reached here that they have taken Shapen's Farm on the North side of the James opposite Drury's Bluff with 3000 of our men prisoners, but I do not believe the report.

*Colonel Stokes returns to the field and later participates in actions attempting to counter the Union seizure of the Weldon Railroad.*

Camp 4th S. C. Cavalry,
Malone's Farm,
July 31st, 1864

We left here about two o'clock before day yesterday on a long foraging expedition on neutral ground between our grounds and that of the enemy. In fact we got some oats within a mile or two of the enemy's pickets. We brought off 18 wagon loads of oats and fifteen head of cattle. When the expedition was about accomplished, the wagons loaded and started off, we heard cannonading on our right, which if the enemy succeeded in taking, and advanced a short distance, would have command of the road we went, so the wagons were sent with a guard to the left of that we went, and General B. took the remainder of the 4th and 5th Regiments which went on the expedition and moved back to the same road we went, (Lt Col Miller of the 6th Regiment was on picket at the post mentioned, Lee['s] Mill, with his Regiment and ordered to hold the place). On arriving at the road leading to the mill, we met some of Lt Col Miller's men saying that Miller and all of his men were captured. We commenced moving in the direction of the mill and when we had gotten about a mile

158

down the road got in rather an ambuscade of the enemy, and both Regiments were thrown in confusion for a few minutes, but they were rallied soon and dismounted in time to repulse a charge from the enemy, capturing two of their men prisoners; one a Lieutenant. Our line then advanced and drove the enemy back. Our Regiment lost one man killed and two wounded. They belonged to Calhoun[144] and Breeden's[145] Company. We then returned to camp where we arrived about 11 o'clock P. M. I was in the saddle about 18 hours and rode about 45 to 50 miles. We were ordered down again this morning and rode a few miles and were ordered to return again. The whole Regiment goes on picket tomorrow, though I do not expect to go. I will meet with the examining board. Lt Col Miller was not captured; he escaped by a road to the right, but lost nearly all the horses that were being led for two Squadrons and some twenty or twenty-five men.

I had forgotten to say that the wagons and cattle all got into camp safe, but upon the whole I think it very dearly bought.

Capt Barber has returned to camp, but is still unwell.

Monday Morning,
August 1st, 1864

It is reported that Sheridan is again on the move in the direction of Stoney Creek and our whole division has orders to be ready to move at a moment's notice. All the other Cavalry has gone on the north side of the James. It is thought they intend to try to cut the R.R. again. I will not meet the board, but go with the command if the whole goes.

Camp 4th S. C. Cav.
Webb's Farm,
August 4, 1864

We moved today to a new camp, about two miles from the old one and that much nearer the R.R. The move was principally to get a clean camp and to get clear of the *flies* which was perfectly awful and I am sorry to say that quite a number of

159

them are here already; still they are everywhere in Va. that I have been yet. The woods seem to be full of them. This is a very nice place for a camp.

While writing the above, I overheard Col R. in conversation with Capt Barber say that "I want to see another star on that man's [referring to me] collar; he deserves it," which . . . will show you his appreciation of my action out here, but I claim to have done nothing more than my duty and only state the above that you may know that my conduct has been noticed by others. . . .

It seems that the yankees have gotten my name. They told one of our men from Capt McIver's Co., whom they captured at Trevilian and left on their retreat near Bowling Green very ill, and who got back a few days ago, says the yankees told him that Col Stokes was wounded. Fortunately for me they were mistaken.

Camp 4th S. C. Cavalry,
Web[b]'s Farm, Va.
August 5, 1864

I am sorry to say that the horses in the Regiment are generally in a deplorable condition. They only get enough feed to keep them at what they are and they are certainly low enough. A large number of the worst have been sent to the Valley of Virginia, where they ought to recruit very fast. Col R. has certainly not taken any steps yet to get the Regiment back to the coast, but I think he is very tired of Virginia, and would like very much or would not have the slightest objection to return to the coast.

General Lee has not gone to Hood's[146] Army.

Camp 4th S. C. Cavalry,
Web[b]'s Farm, Va.
August 7th, 1864

Col R. has gone on picket again today with four squadrons of the Regiment (8 Cos.). I escaped it again by being on the examining Board. Capt A.'s squadron is the only one left.

I expect to get through with the Board as far as we can, for a while, this week; then I will be on hand on every occasion, for Col R. does not love work much.

The report here is that Mobile, Ala.,[147] has fallen, but I hope it is not true. The enemy have been remarkably quiet here and around Petersburgh during the past few days, but I do not see how they could be otherwise owing to the extremely warm weather.

I expect a lot of Capt A.'s men will go home on horse details sometime this week.

Camp 4th S. C. Cavalry,
Web[b]'s Farm, Va.
August 9th, 1864

The news from Petersburgh is that Grant is moving his heavy guns to City Point.

I hear that Longstreet's Corps has been sent off.

I have just heard that General Butler is or intends making a desperate effort to get our Regiment sent to the Coast of S. C. as soon as the summer campaign is over. How he will succeed you can guess as near as I can. One thing is certain, the Brigade is very much used up and will never recruit here and if we are sent to So. Car. during the winter and get plenty of feed we can recruit and be able to return again next spring *if necessary.*

Wednesday Morning,
August 10th, 1864

Three of Capt Pinckney's[148] men deserted the other day and it is thought that they went to the enemy, though some think they have gone home. They are the same men that were caught with dogs[149] last winter and were tried and sentenced to be shot and the President reprieved them so you can see the folly of remitting the sentence of such rascals. These men were cut off when the companies were reduced and they were sent out here under guard about two weeks [ago].

Camp 4th S. C. Cavalry,
near Richmond, Va.
August 12th, 1864

I am surprised at the report about I. M. Liston. I have not heard anything of the kind intimated here. He has only been under fire with me once since I have had him as horseholder and then I am glad to say that I saw nothing like cowardice in him. In fact he acted very well indeed during the action. General Butler wanted a mounted man and had none and I told him to take Isaac to a place out on one of the flanks as a vidette[150] to watch for the enemy and he gave full satisfaction.

I hear Genl H. has been placed in command of all the Cavalry in the A.N.V. If so Genl B. will command Genl Hampton's Division and Col R. will be in command of the Brigade. The baggage has been ordered to be reduced this evening and when that is the case here everyone knows what is coming—an active campaign. Still we are taking it easy enough so far. Started at sunrise this morning and stopped at 11 o'clock and will stay here tonight.

Camp 4th S. C. Cavalry,
Malone's Farm,
August 12th, 1864

The order for the movement of the whole command was countermanded and I asked Genl B. if I had better suspend the meeting of the Board and go with the Regiment on picket and he said not [to] suspend its meeting to go on picket.

General F. H. Lee's Division of Cavalry has returned and our duty will not be so hard any more, I hope.

Have heard nothing more of the movements of Sheridan. The report that Frasier's Farm had fallen with a loss of 3000 prisoners was false.

Camp 4th S. C. Cavalry,
South Anna, North Side,
August 13, 1864

We marched some 23 miles on yesterday and encamped on
the river near where the R.R. crosses it, at the same place where
we did the first day we marched from Richmond to report.

I hear that we are going to Culpepper[151] Co. The weather is
very warm and dry and the marches are very fatiguing and our
meals very irregular.

I have no men to command. The whole Division moved
through Richmond in regular order. Quite a long line it was
and the wagon train was about two miles long. I wrote you
that General H. had been placed in command of all the Cavalry.
Genl B. is in command of the Division and Col R. is in command of the Brigade at present, but I hear it positively asserted
that Col Dunovant is to be made a Brig. Gen. in a day or two
and placed in command of our Brigade. I believe it will be
done. Col R. is very much mortified at it, he being Col D.'s
Senior.

Camp 4th S. C. Cavalry near
Ashland, Va.
August 15th, 1864

We are now some twenty miles back on our way to Richmond, some sixteen miles above the latter place on the
R.[ichmond] and Fredericksburg R.R. The enemy have made
a strong demonstration below Richmond on the north side and
we received orders last night while on the North Anna and are
making a forced march back.

We are here awaiting further orders, the whole Division,
and do not know whether the orders will be for us to go on
down below R.[ichmond] or turn back on our march to
Culpepper Court House.

I hear that the enemy's Cavalry crossed at Bottom's Bridge
yesterday or today and whipped Genl Gary's[152] Brigade, which
consisted of the old Hampton Legion, 7th S. C. and 26th Va.
Cavalry Regiments.

163

Camp 4th S. C. Cavalry
near Savage Station,
York R.R., Virginia.
August 17th, 1864

We are in two miles of Bottom's Bridge. We went down to where they were fighting near Chaffin's Farm yesterday, with the expectation of going in, but reinforcements had arrived and they were driving them back when we got there and our Brigade was held in reserve for several hours and then ordered here last night. Jenkins' Brigade was in the fight. I was in a mile of it, some one told me, but could not leave my Regiment to go to it. Col R. is still in command of the Brigade. We captured a number of prisoners, among them one negro. The negroes I heard drove back Jenkins' Brigade[153] at first, but they soon rallied and slaughtered them afterwards. A great many whites were killed also. Our loss was small. General Chambliss,[154] commanding a Va. Cavalry Brigade, was killed on our side.

It is thought that Grant intends to try his hands on this side [of] the river again, and we will remain here for several days at least I think to watch and picket the left flank of the enemy.

Camp 4th S. C. Cavalry
near  Savage Station,
August 19th, 1864

We went down on yesterday to attack the enemy some four miles below. A general attack was to have been made all along the line from here to the James, directed by Genl R. E. Lee, but the signal for our portion of the line to commence the attack was not given until 4 P. M. when it was to have been given at 11 A. M. So we attacked and drove the enemy back until dark, but there was very little attack on any other portion of the line as well as I could hear. I do not know why it was postponed. We captured one Capt and eight or nine men. The Captain was dressed up like a dandy. We are ordered to move the camp this morning somewhere over toward the James, and my Regiment is saddled up ready to move. No one was hurt in the Regiment yesterday.

164

Camp 4th S. C. Cavalry
near White's Tavern,
Charles City Road, Seven
Miles Below Richmond
August 21st, 1864

We are ordered to move forward to feel the enemy. Their Infantry have fallen back. We leave in a few minutes.

We only went about half a mile when we were halted and turned back. The enemy's Cavalry and all had gone to the South Side so we have orders to recross the James also.

I expect the grand battle will come off now, or rather I would not be surprised if it did. There has been a good deal of fighting the past three or four days.

Camp 4th S. C. Cavalry
on Gravel[ly] Run,
Near Reams Station,
August 24th, 1864

We had a pretty sharp fight again on yesterday, but I was not in it as Genl Butler had sent me off to establish the picket line of the Division, with six squadrons of Cavalry. A pretty dangerous business it was and I came near being cut off by the advancing enemy. I got to the fight just after it commenced and was ordered by Genl Butler to guard an important road on his right. We drove the enemy about two miles and took two lines of their works. Night ended the fight. Our Regiment lost some eight or ten killed and wounded, none hurt in Appleby's Company. I. Liston was struck on the elbow with a spent ball and just deadened his arm for a while; the skin is not broken. The enemy's line has advanced some two or three miles further than it ever was before. I look for pretty active times for the next ten days.

P. S. The enemy hold the P.& W. R.R. from near Petersburgh to Reams Station, about eight miles.

On Out Post Seven Miles
Below Petersburgh
August 27th, 1864

You will see from the above that I am on picket duty and am in command of a line about four miles long. I was ordered here on yesterday, with our Regiment and one from Young's[155] Brigade for forty-eight hours. Do you know that it is the first time I have ever been regularly on picket since I have been in the War.

I have spent a good portion of the day on the lines. The enemy's lines are about one mile from my Head Quarters. The picketing on the coast is nothing to that here.

We had a heavy battle at the Reams Station on Thursday last. Had A. P. Hill's[156] Corps to assist the Cavalry. Hill cut through their lines on the right of their works and the Cavalry attacked them on the left, completely surrounded them and captured something over 3,000 prisoners besides the killed and wounded. Our Brigade was not engaged, one Regiment, the 5th, was on picket and the other portion did not have their horses fed for two days and were sent back to feed. We were sent on the field next day to gather up the plunder arms, etc. and I never saw the like of arms, etc., dead horses and men in my life.

Head Quarters Out Post
on Vaughan's Road,
Seven Miles Below
Petersburgh, Va.
August 28th, 1864

Capt McCurry has asked and is to be relieved from duty with the Regiment in a few days and expects to be assigned some duty in South Carolina. He is not generally liked as Army Quartermaster in the Regiment is why I suppose he has applied for duty elsewhere.

It is very discouraging to Officers who brought out such a Regiment as ours, numbering some seven or eight hundred effective horses to be able to report only some seventy-five or eighty effective horses for duty and the greater portion of them it would be dangerous to undertake to charge on. The great work we have accomplished is very plain to be seen and is admitted generally.

Maj Morgan, 5th S. C. Cavalry, was shot in the heel of the foot in last Wednesday's fight and his leg had to be cut off a little above the ankle. You know he was shot in the other foot at Pocotaligo. He has certainly been unfortunate. He is in fine spirits and says he will be back in three months.

Monday Morning,
August 29th, 1864

Another horse detail is to be sent off in a few days. General D.[157] seems to be using every effort to try to recruit the army up again. I hope he may be successful. General R. E. Lee is very much pleased with the action of the Cavalry. He published a very complimentary order of them a few days ago.[158] The best of it is that the fighting of the Cavalry dates only from about the time our Brigade arrived here. It fought so obstinately and so unlike any Cavalry heretofore that the others became inspired on account of State pride to do likewise. One man in Rosser's[159] Brigade, which was fighting on the left of ours, on coming out said to one of his comrades, "It is no use to deny it—Butler's Brigade can out fight any troops on foot in the Army of Northern Virginia."

*The battles continued into September. Because the Union forces still occupied a portion of the Weldon Railroad, food supplies became critical. General Hampton launched a raid on September 14, in the rear of Grant's base at City Point, which alleviated the food problem for a while. In addition to assessing the strength of the Regiment, Colonel Stokes relates some interesting details of Hampton's raid.*

Camp 4th S. C. Cavalry,
Gravel[ly] Run,
August 30, 1864

Things have been very quiet around here since the fight at Reams Station. I will go on picket in two more days with my

167

Regiment. Col R. is president of a courts martial which of course will take him away from the command of the Regiment for some time. The mounted portion of it now is not more than a Captain's command.

> Camp 4th S. C. Cavalry,
> Army Northern Va.,
> Gravel[ly] Run,
> Sept 2nd, 1864

We are under marching orders to move at a moment's notice. The enemy are reported as moving on the South Side R.R. which is about some ten or twelve miles to the northwest of this place.

I am again put on the examining board. We will meet in a few days if we do not have to run about after the yanks. Our Regiment reported this morning only nine Com. Officers and eighty enlisted men. The total number of the Regiment mounted and dismounted, present and absent, is 903, also including those in the hands of the enemy, so you can see how near our Regiment is played out. And the other Regiments in the Brigade are about in the same fix.

> Camp 4th S. C. Cavalry,
> Boydton Plank Road,
> Sept 6th, 1864

We have moved camp again. We are now on the Plank Road eight miles from Petersburg. The Plank Road runs from Petersburgh to Dinwiddie Court House. The fight at Reams Station was a big one, but the loss in the Cavalry was very small. The Cavalry is not what it used to be in this army. It stands high and is so acknowledged by every branch of the service.

I do not think we can dislodge the enemy entirely from the Weldon R.R. without costing us more than it is worth. Scouts report that they are massing in our front, Infantry, Cavalry and Artillery, with a view of making a raid on the south side of the R.R. which is not more than five miles from our vidette line. I think we are pretty well prepared for them.

Camp 4th S. C. Cavalry
Boydton Plank Road,
near Petersburgh
Sept 8th, 1864

The two armies still confront each other with little or no change. Deserters are coming in constantly under General Order no. 65 from the War Department promising to send them through our lines to their homes: those who have been drafted or forced into the service against their wishes and are tired of it. Two came in a few days ago to my videttes.

Dr G.[160] is still sick and the Medical Board has recommended a forty days furlough for him. I suppose it will be returned in a day or two when he will leave for home. Capt A. has sent up a very strong application for thirty days to see after his father's estate and I expect he will get it. Lt Berry will be sent on a horse detail in a few days also.

Camp 4th S. C. Cavalry,
Boydton Plank Road, Va.,
Sept 10th, 1864

I have just returned from Petersburgh and find that Dr Gregory leaves on his sick furlough in the morning.

The enemy charged our picket lines near Petersburgh last night and took a portion of them through false pretenses, representing themselves as deserters, but they were soon retaken.

Camp 4th S. C. Cavalry,
Boydton Plank Road,
Sept 16th, 1864

I did not go with General Hampton on that cattle expedition. The order was countermanded and only a few men and one lieutenant were sent. I would almost as soon have gone for we have been out after the enemy every day since. Yesterday the enemy drove in our pickets and advanced about two miles and then retired to their old line. Today we drove in theirs and advanced to their strong works and retired without getting a man in the Brigade shot. I was sent down yesterday to reestablish our post with my Regiment and succeeded in doing so without getting any one hurt. Our movement today was to divert their attention from Genl H., but I am afraid from the information we got from a prisoner that was captured that they already have a column after him. Should such be the case we will be sent to his relief immediately. I left the Regiment on picket today and returned with Genl D.[unovant] to show him some of the roads, etc. and on arriving here we met Genl Robt. E. Lee whom Genl D. introduced me to. He called on me to point out to the General on his map the different points that he wanted information about and which Genl D. knew but little about.

> Camp 4th S. C. Cavalry,
> Boydton Plank Road,
> Sept 18th, 1864

The enemy sent a large force to intercept Genl H. as Genl Young and Dunovant went with all the Cavalry to assist him, except what was on picket, my Regiment being one. Genl Young placed me in command of the whole Cavalry line of pickets and dismounted men of the various Brigades with orders to report any movement of the enemy directly to General Lee.

They returned yesterday evening. Genl H. had met the force of the enemy, whipped them and got all of this plunder safe before Genl Young joined him. Genl H. got 2500 head of fine beef cattle, five wagons, thirty-five mules and about 200 horses.

General Hampton's route was as follows: by Reams Station and then down the Petersburgh and Jerusalem Plank Road, then across the Norfolk and P. R.R. and the Black Water River to Cabin Point on the James River near where Prince George joins it in Sussex County. Grant's army extends from within two or three miles of Reams Station to near Warwick's Wharf on the north side of the James. The enemy attacked Genl H. on the Jerusalem P.[lank] R.[oad] and while he was fighting them his plunder crossed the Nottaway River and went on to Stoney Creek, leaving Genl H.'s whole force between them

170

and the enemy. When night came on Genl H. withdrew after driving the yanks back some distance and followed his cattle, etc., and the Yanks followed the back track. Some seventy prisoners were captured in the engagement and some two hundred and fifty with the cattle besides a large amount of stores were burnt. We only lost some ten men killed and a few wounded. It is certainly one of the most brilliant feats of the war.

*Fighting continued through the rest of September and the entire month of October with Hampton's Cavalry administering severe punishment to the Union forces at Hatcher's Run and on the Vaughan and Squirrel Level Roads. Because of further action at Hatcher's Run, there was a terrific battle at Burgess' Mill on October 27. Colonel Stokes and his men were among those that forced Grant to withdraw into his own lines after his failure to reach the end of the Confederate fortifications.*

Camp 4th S. C. Cavalry,
Boydton Plank Road,
Sept 20th, 1864

Capt A. is on picket with the Regiment now. The duty is very hard. We go every third day. I seldom go out any more on picket except on a special occasion on account of being on the examining board, but continue in command of the Regiment all the time notwithstanding. I am off on examining board about as often as Col R. is on the courts martial.

Camp 4th S. C. C.
Burgess Mill, Boydton P.R.
Sept 25th, 1864

I have just returned from Church at Dinwiddie C.[ourt] H.[ouse] some 7 miles, heard a very good sermon from an Episcopal minister. It is the first that I have heard in a long, long time and I hope I will be much benefited by it.

Yesterday I dined with Genl D– and in the evening Capt Davis, 5th S.C.C., and myself went up to Mrs. Gilham to pay her and her daughter a visit; they live 7 miles from here and had sent me several messages to come to see them. They gave us a very nice supper and we spent a very pleasant evening, for two married men, which the ladies were well aware of. I was delighted with the number on the Piano by a Miss Thomas, of Fairfax Co., a refugee, also with her history of her imprisonment by the yankees in 1861 in the old capitol at Washington. Her house is not far from Mason's Hill and when the enemy were driven back, her mother & herself got in a carriage and undertook to go there and the first thing they knew, they were in the hands of a party of yankee pickets who took them to Washington & they were kept there for some time as spies. She is a very fine and intelligent lady and I think the most patriotic lady that I have met with in Va; says that she would prefer dying in the trenches fighting than to give up our cause.

Camp 4th S. C. Cavalry,
Burgess' Mill,
Sept 27th, 1864

Genl Rosser's Brigade of our Division left this morning to reinforce Early.

Camp 4th S. C. C.
Burgess' Mill,
Sept 29th, 1864

. . . . I am going on picket today. . . . The news from the Valley is encouraging. Genl Early has struck bottom and staked down again at least for a while I hope. I suppose the low spirited people are enlivened again.

It is very dry here now but looks like rain this morning, but I would like to see it continue dry until I get off picket. The duty is very heavy now. The men are out every third night, though I do not expect to go on only every sixth night.

Col R– is having a very pleasant time at Dinwiddie C.[ourt] H.[ouse] on the Courts Martial. He has lost ground both in the Regt and with his superior officers. . . . I am sorry of it. A friend told me that Col R. told him that he heard that Genl B– in referring to me one day said "that is *the man* of the 4th

172

S.C.C." and that he would like very much to know what he had done to draw forth such a remark. I will not say more, but hope I may be able to be with you before many more days when I can talk freely of such matters.

Burgess' Mill,
Oct 2nd, 1864

The enemy were reported as advancing the day I left for picket, and [I] re-established our post after a sharp fight. I remained on picket that night, but did not get my line re-established until about ten o'clock P. M. The next day they advanced on me about ten A. M. and I fought them with a handful of men for three hours when I was forced to retire before an overwhelming force, falling back on some breast works where Genl D. was. Our little force could not hold their own against two yankee Corps and Genl D. withdrew to prevent a flank movement. We were marching and counter-marching nearly all that night and yesterday a general attack was made on the enemy which was commenced at daylight and lasted all day through a drenching rain. The fight was very stubborn all day and particularly so in the evening when we charged them and took all of their works except one strong fort which was near our line. At dark we withdrew our line. Our Brigade made two charges against it and in the first attack was unsuccessful. I regret to say our gallant and worthy Genl Dunovant was shot through the brain near me and Genl Butler who was near by ordered me to take command of the Brigade, which I did, and bring them forward until the whole line was forced to give back a little under the most obstinate fire I have ever been in, but I soon rallied them and held the place under a terrific fire half an hour until ordered to retire.

The bullets were about equal to the Hawes' Shop fight with an addition of grape and shell.

Serg. Risher was shot in the left leg, and it had to be amputated. William Risher went to take him home. No other in Capt A.'s Company was shot. The loss in the Brigade was only thirty-eight killed, wounded and missing (about seven killed and two missing).

173

We lost only one killed and four wounded in our Regiment on Saturday.

The death of General Dunovant was a great loss to the Brigade and is deeply regretted by both Officers and men. I regret Serg. Risher's losing his leg. His loss is irreparable to his Company.

I forgot to tell you that a ball passed through my new overcoat which I had on.

Bivouac 4th S. C. Cavalry,
Armstrong Mill,
Hatcher's Run,
October 4th, 1864

We have not had any more fighting since Saturday, but have been kept out here near the line in readiness in case another movement of the enemy should take place, though we expect to be relieved this evening or tomorrow sometime.

Our Serg. Maj. Benton I regret to say was painfully wounded in the hand on Saturday and has gone to Raleigh, N. C. hospital and I suppose will go home from there. He is a good fellow and I shall miss his services.

There has been some fighting on the north side, but I have heard little of the particulars except that Grant was severely punished. They have advanced their lines about one mile on this side, but have gained nothing and given us a much better line; besides they paid very dearly for that mile and our loss was small. A deserter came in this morning and said that his colonel said that Grant had said that he did not intend to unsaddle his horse until he took Richmond. I imagine he will be saddled some time.

Bivouac at Armstrong Mill,
October 6th, 1864

We are still in bivouac at this place, but will move to camp today. The camp has been changed from the Plank Road to Gravel[ly] Run near where we were before we went to the Plank Road, but not near[ly] so pleasant a place.

174

Friday, October 7th, 1864

We are in camp again. Col R. is at the Brigade Head
Quarters.

Camp 4th S. C. Cavalry
near Armstrong Mill,
October 9th, 1864

The enemy advanced a short distance yesterday in the
direction of the South Side R.R. and a fight was expected
today, but they returned again last night.

The enemy have been severely punished on the north side,
but at a great loss to us.

Cols R. and Aiken are both running for Brig. General.

Camp 4th S. C. Cavalry
near Armstrong Mill,
October 11th, 1864

I heard heavy firing last night and early this morning in
the direction of the north side.  Expect they have had another
fight over there.  We have been disappointed in not having a
fight here before this, though we do not regret it.  They have
withdrawn their lines a little in our front.

Wm. Risher has returned.  The Serg. on the Weldon R.R.
would not let him take Sergt. R. on, but sent him to Wilson
Hospital somewhere on the line of R.R.

Camp Butler's Brigade,
near Armstrong Mill,
October 14th, 1864

Yesterday I was engaged all day on the Examining Board.
Dr Fontaine was killed, when going to see General D. after he
was shot, by a shell.  He was the Medical Director of the Cavalry Corps of the A. N. V.

Col R.'s court-martial has been dissolved for the present and
he is still in command of the Brigade.

General Butler has made an application for this Brigade to
be sent back to So. Car. and the 1st, 2nd, and 3rd, to take our

175

places, on the ground that it will be for the good of the service, owing to the condition of our horses. Genl B– thinks it will be done and that we will leave here on or about the first of December. The men have heard something of it, but do not know the truth, nor does Genl B– want them to know, for fear it may not be done.

Camp Butler's Brigade,<br>Armstrong Mill, Va.<br>October 16th, 1864

General H. and staff were not captured. In fact, I do not believe they have been on the North Side since we left them sometime ago.

Camp Butler's Brigade,<br>Armstrong Mill.<br>October 18th, 1864

The two contending armies are still the same. Those on the North Side are busily engaged in fortifying, I suppose. We have Hatcher's Run on this side very well fortified, and if the Yanks undertake to advance on the South Side R.R. we will give them a warm reception.

There is heavy cannonading tonight on the North Side, but nothing very unusual.

Camp Butler's Cavalry<br>Brigade, Armstrong Mill,<br>October 20th, 1864

A small demonstration was made by the enemy this morning on Genl Dearing's[161] Brigade but was immediately checked.

The order countermanding details is being pretty rigidly enforced here.[162] It is increasing the army some. We do not care how many come, the more the better.

Col Aiken returned this evening and I suppose Col R will either return to his Regiment or convene the court-martial again. Capt Appleby has gone to the Danville Hospital.

Camp Butler, Cavalry Brigade
October 23rd, 1864

Early has been whipped again in the Valley.

Col A. has not reported for duty yet. He has been unwell since his arrival.

Camp Butler
on Quaker Road,
October 25th, 1864

Genl R. E. Lee has issued an order, returning all able bodied detailed clerks, couriers, forage masters, etc. in all Offices and departments in the A. N. V. to their companies at once and putting light duty men in their places. How the fine dressed couriers at General's Head Quarters and other places do hate it. The order is strictly carried out here and the increase is wonderful.

Col Aiken is now in command of the Brigade. Lieut Col Jeffords is here in command of his Regiment.

We moved camp today after a mile in the direction of the Plank Road and to where we can get plenty of wood. It is called Camp Butler. We will not suffer here for the want of wood for several months.

Rhett is acting Sergeant-Major during the absence of Benton, who was wounded in the hand on October 1st.

Camp Butler,
October 28th, 1864

I have passed through another severe battle through the Mercy of God safely.

The enemy made a grand advance on the South Side R.R. yesterday morning and took our line of works about daylight before we had time to man them and advanced with us fighting them until we reached the Boydton Plank Road, our present encampment falling into their hands, though they got nothing valuable. We concentrated on them on the Plank Road and gave them a decent whipping and they retreated to their old position last night. We captured a number of prisoners, but

177

could we have had about two hours more of daylight we would have captured about one half their force. We are now occupying our old camp and I hope they have sufficient warning not to try us soon again. The fight was severe in the extreme, but the old 4th did its work nobly, especially the left of the line which was under my immediate command, consisting of Capt A.'s Squadron under Lieut Berry, and Calhoun's Squadron under Capt Breeden. Capt A.'s Company went in with nine men and had four wounded: Wm. Hiers, pretty badly on the shoulder (flesh); Wm. Byrd, slightly on the shoulder (flesh); Wm Canady, a very serious wound on the shoulder; Hickman, a slight wound on the hip. The old Company fought well and I feel proud of it. We took in the fight about forty or fifty men and got one killed and about fifteen or twenty wounded. The other portion of the Regiment was on picket.

Saturday, October 29th, 1864

After the fighting was over on Thursday night, or after it got so dark we could not see how to fight, I was left with seventy-five (75) men and three pieces of Artillery to vidette and command the Out Post.

Lieut Col Jeffords was killed, shot through the heart. Lieut Wade Hampton, Genl H.'s son, was killed and his other son,[163] a Lieut on his Staff, was severely wounded. We had but little protection is why our loss was so great, but it was mostly in wounded. I was in on horse back again and the bullets cut me very close frequently, but through the blesing of God I came out safe.

P. S. The enemy's force was four Divisions of Infantry with Cavalry and Artillery. We fought them with about three or four thousand (3 or 4000) of all branches.

Camp Butler, A. N. V.,
October 30th, 1864

I promised to give you a detailed account of the fight. From two of their surgeons who were left in charge of about sixty of their wounded that they were not able to take off in their hasty retreat we have learned that it is one of their greatest defeats of the war. They came out with three corps of Infantry and a Brigade of Cavalry and Artillery in proportion. About two thirds of the Infantry with a greater portion of the Artillery and all of the Cavalry broke through our lines on the south side of Hatcher's Run and we (the Cavalry) gave them a running fight until we got back to the Plank Road which we were forced to do owing to the number of roads they were advancing by and the scattered condition of our Cavalry. We concentrated on the Plank Road and stopped their advance and commenced very soon to beat them back with the assistance of some of the Infantry. But night closed in too soon and they got off in the darkness of the night, leaving all of their dead and a great many wounded and other things. The other one third of the yankee force attacked our dismounted men on the other side of Hatcher's Run behind breast works on the right of our Infantry and were repulsed there. At that place our Regiment lost one killed and one wounded. Paul Spell was the one that was killed. The total loss in the Regiment was two killed and twelve wounded and three captured. We fought the enemy all through our present camp and one lieutenant and two men of the 6th Regiment and a man of Young's Brigade were killed near our Head Quarters. The fighting of the Brigade was good and the loss very lamentable.

Capt A. has returned from the Danville Hospital yesterday. I have heard of the death of Sergt. Risher.

Monday Morning,
November 1st, 1864

The fight on Thursday, 27th, was the fifteenth fight I have been in since we came out.

*The letters for the year 1864 close with a raid on Stoney Creek Station and Belfield, near the North Carolina line. The weather has turned colder, and with the dimmer light of winter, the waning of the Confederacy grew more ominous.*

179

Camp Butler, A. N. V.
November 5th, 1864

The report is that Grant has recrossed his army from the North Side to this again, which I suppose is true as Genl Lee has moved his Head Quarters down in this vicinity. He usually has his Head Quarters where he expects the most active work.

Below Petersburgh, Virginia,
November 8th, 1864

We were ordered to saddle up on yesterday and expected to have another round with the Yanks, but their demonstration was very small and they soon retired to their old position, so we have again quieted down.
The enemy are very quiet.

P. S. All quiet this morning.

Camp Butler,
November 10, 1864

A number of the Officers are getting out their wives here. Genl B.'s is here, also Capt Gregg's. They have to pay enormous board for them.

Camp Butler A. N. V.
November 13th, 1864

We have heard nothing definite from the yankee Presidential election,[164] but all believe that Old Abe is elected. . . . I hear saying he is elected & that they do not mean to fight any more. Two cavalrymen came over here yesterday, bringing horses and everything and said that half of their Co. wanted to come, but I place very little reliance in deserter's tales. . . .

Camp Butler, A. N. V.,
November 14th, 1864

All is quiet this morning.

Camp Butler,
Nov. 17th, 1864

My leave was not approved by Genl Lee. Genl H.[ampton], I think killed it by approving it when "active operations cease. . ." I regret exceedingly not getting the leave but submit to it like a good soldier.

Col R's Court is again in session and they have Capts Barker & Appleby on it with him which I think will somewhat reduce my chances [for a leave] until they get through. I rather think that Genl Lee expects a great battle between this and the 1st Dec. If it has to come I expect it won't come very soon.

Camp Butler,
Nov 20th/64

It has been raining a slow rain since Friday night and the clouds are still low & thick, but little water has fallen; still the woods must be very sloppy and bad as it takes but little rain to put them in that condition. There is not enough to stop military operations but will impede it somewhat. I hope it will continue on until there is enough to end the campaign, if that will end it, for I think I have done enough fighting for one year. Besides, by its going on, I do not think there is anything for us to gain by it. Should Grant make his desperate attack on Richmond & we repulse him, he will fall back behind his works & we cannot dislodge him with our force and he may then change "his base" farther south, which I should regret very much to see done.

Sherman's move in Ga seems to be persisting & I am very much afraid he will make for Charleston or Savannah, notwithstanding I believe he will have a "hard road to travel." Still, he might possibly succeed in making the trip and devastate the whole country through which he passes, which is about all that he could take time to do.

181

Camp Butler,
Nov. 22nd/64

[I read] a Richmond paper this morning from the Northern extracts in which it seems that a *dishonorable peace* will be proposed or may be proposed by Old Abe, that is to come back into this *accursed Union* again and I am very fearful that some of our people will be foolish enough to entertain it, thusly causing a division of sentiment in the confederacy, which will ruin us forever, & destroy our cause; may *God* have *mercy* upon us as a nation and direct our *destiny*, is our prayer.

Sherman I see is on the wing & has cut the R.R. 25 miles below Macon. Should he get to Augusta & start for Charleston you had better get out of the way. . . .

Camp Butler,
November 24th, 1864

General Young with the dismounted men of the Division, about 500 strong, is going on to Augusta, Georgia, to aid in the defence of that place and then procure horses and return. We will send forty-seven (47) men from our Regiment and about one hundred and fifty (150) from the Brigade.

I hear that there was a pretty severe engagement on the James River today and that we repulsed the enemy. We expect one here any day.

Camp Butler,
November 27th, 1864

Col R. and Capts Barber and Appleby have been out there at the Court House for the past twelve or fifteen days on that Court Martial and for the last ten days have not had a quorum, consequently have been there doing nothing at all that time and are very likely to remain there for the next week in the same condition.

Monday,
November 28th, 1864

Genl Butler inspected the horses of our Regiment on Saturday and condemned and pronounced unserviceable some eighty odd. The condemned are to be sold. The unserviceable are to be sent to the recruiting camp in Lancaster Dist., So. Car., to recruit. It only leaves us with sixty-three privates for duty with serviceable horses.

Camp Butler, A. N. V.,
November 29th, 1864

Everything has been very quiet here for some time.

I have just heard of the death of Junius Risher, through both Wm. R. and I. Liston.

Our wounded officers and men are coming in occasionally. Four or five officers have returned within the past month. Capt McIver,[165] who was wounded both in the foot and arm severely at the Hawes Shop fight, came in two days ago. I consider him about the best officer of his rank both in the Regiment or the Brigade. The horses that were condemned as unserviceable the other day left here today for Stoney Creek preparatory to going to South Carolina to be recruited. We have left in the Regiment only some sixty-three (63) privates and fifteen or twenty non-commissioned officers mounted for duty and some ten or twelve officers, a Regiment in name only.

Wednesday,
November 30th, 1864

There is some movement on the part of the yankees this morning. I suppose they are advancing. We are saddling up to meet them.

Camp Butler, A. N. V.,
December 2nd, 1864

A column of the enemy moved against Stoney Creek, where we get all of our supplies on yesterday morning and, I under-

183

stand, either burned or caused us to burn all that was there and captured about 125 of the garison which consisted of some 350 or 300 Cavalry men with unserviceable horses.

Our Division started down about four o'clock yesterday evening to intercept them, but they had gone and we lay out all night (what portion who were not traveling) and found we were too late, that we could do nothing, and returned to camp about ten o'clock this morning, very much fatigued and sleepy and hungry. Genl Wm. F. H. Lee's Cavalry Division was encamped some eight miles from the station and his pickets cover that point. He engaged the enemy slightly after they had done all the damage and followed them some distance. General Butler sent me down on Wednesday, the day before it occurred, to within three miles of the station to select a camping ground for the Division, where we expect to go into winter quarters and be convenient to our supplies, for it will be almost impossible to run a wagon train there if the roads get much worse and it is eighteen miles. I selected a very good camp and we were to have moved tomorrow, but I expect we will be delayed now until sometime next week, as I have heard nothing of the move since my return to camp.

I have just got the result of our loss at Stoney Creek Station. The total number of men and officers are about 175. Of this number there are 56 men and three officers of our Regiment, seven from Capt A.'s Company: J. J. Folk, Sam Goodwin, V. C. Kinsey, Henry Vaughan, Wm. McAlhany, Henry Strickland and Robert Johnston. Capt Walthouer of Young's Ga Cavalry Brigade was in command of the Post and is said to be a very good and gallant officer.

Saturday Morning,
December 3rd, 1864

We got the order late last night to move camp to near Stoney Creek Depot at 7 o'clock this morning. We will be in some three or four miles of the station.

184

Camp near Stoney Creek
Station, Sussex Co., Virginia,
December 4th, 1864

I think we will make our new camp very comfortable, should
Mr. Grant permit us to occupy it as winter quarters as our Generals intend us to do. The ground is very broken; consequently
the camp is laid off and the nature of the ground would permit
but little system.[?]

We had quite a novel occurrence in camp this morning. A
lot of about twelve (12) turkeys (wild) was flushed by some one
and they came flying over and some few shots were fired at
them and they lit about between the different Regiments of the
Brigade and commenced to run. The men took after them with
a yelling and two were killed and five run down by the men of
my Regiment alone.

Grant's troops had their big turkey dinner that was sent
them from the North the other day and we will have ours
tomorrow.

Camp near Stony Creek
Dec. 6th, 1864

We have no news here except a report this evening that the
enemy cavalry had gone down in the direction of Weldon,
N. C. and that we were ordered to go meet them. I hardly
think it more than a camp rumor.

I have heard a good many of the particulars of the fight at
Grahamville from a member of the C.[harleston] L.[ight]
D.[ragoons] just from So. Car. Col R– thinks that the courts
martial will be through in about one week more with their
business, so if my leave does not get off before, they cannot
certainly refuse granting it then. I have almost come to the
conclusion that an equivalent to a promotion is offered to poor
& conscript officers out here in the way of putting them off out
of the way, thereby giving them an easy time.

Belfield, Virginia,
on the Weldon, R.R.,
December 9th, 1864

The enemy are making a raid with Infantry, Cavalry and Artillery in heavy force against Weldon, N. C. and we have been marching day and night to beat them here and have succeeded in doing so with about 4000 Cavalry and twelve pieces of artillery.

The enemy are now skirmishing with one out post about three miles distant, though we do not expect a general engagement before tomorrow morning. We have some good work and a river, the Mahuing,[166] between us and them; and we expect to repulse them. We have one Corps of Infantry coming on which I suppose will reach here tonight. A. P. Hill's Corps and train has just come in. We have some Militia.

I engaged the enemy slightly with my Regiment yesterday. Did not lose any one, but one wounded in Co."A", Capt McIver's, in the arm.

Camp near Stoney Creek,
Sussex Co., Va.
December 12th, 1864

We were out four days and nights on the Belfield trip and had but two days' rations with us.

The enemy unfortunately found out our force and that we had Infantry as well, and they did not attack us on Saturday morning, but began to retreat about twelve o'clock Friday night, contrary to the expectation of everyone, at such a rapid rate in the sleet that our Infantry could never overtake them and the Cavalry could not reach them until late Saturday evening, nearly night, and we could do nothing at night. Besides they were too strong for the Cavalry to attack alone, so they got back with a few killed and wounded and the loss of a few prisoners.

We just reached here on Saturday evening and have got up our tents and are quite comfortable.

Had the enemy fought us Saturday we would certainly have brought the whole part to grief. There has been another

186

attempt to reach the South Side R.R. and [they] were repulsed, but have heard none of the particulars, except that they were repulsed.

I heard this evening that the camp was to be moved to Belfield on account of getting forage for the horses. The enemy destroyed the R.R. Bridge across the Notaway River[167] and about ten miles of the R.R.

Camp near
Stoney Creek, Virginia,
December 14th, 1864

We leave for Belfield on the Mahuing River tomorrow morning at 7 o'clock. We go there to encamp in order to get forage for the horses, as the recent raid of the enemy so destroyed the R.R. to that point as to prevent the cars from running further than there for the present. I suppose we will not remain there longer than the R.R. can be completed, which may take one month.

We will continue our same picket line near Armstrong Mill on Hatcher's Run which will be about thirty miles from us. Genl Butler received his Major-General's commission today.

Our State may be proud of Hampton and I would not be surprised if Butler did not prove himself an equal after more experience.

Our Division will all go to Belfield tomorrow. It is now Butler's Division instead of Hampton's, but I do not know whose Brigade to call it any more. Aiken's family are very ill and he has gone to Richmond to try to get off to see them. Rutledge is in command of the Brigade.

Thursday Morning,
December 15th, 1864

The order to move today has been countermanded, so I suppose we will remain here for two or three days yet. All quiet.

Camp near Belfield, Virginia,
December 19th, 1864

We have moved down here, (came yesterday) and will soon be comfortably fixed up. I expect we will remain here till the R.R. is repaired which will take at least six weeks or two months, for the yanks did their work effectually. We came down the line of road yesterday. Our camp is the best in all respects that we have ever had since we have been out here.

# 1865

★ ★ ★

*On December 23, 1864, Colonel Stokes was granted a furlough of twenty-one days by General Lee. (See Appendix I, No. 17.) He overstayed his leave by about three weeks (no reason is given) and was placed under arrest until late March, 1865. In the interim, Butler's Cavalry Division, on January 19, 1865, was ordered to South Carolina. Sherman began his march northward, and it was just a matter of when the Confederacy would admit that it had had enough.*

Camp near Columbia, S. C.,
Feb. 2/65

Genl Butler has required me to make out a written statement in regard to overstaying my time, which I have done, but do not know whether it will be satisfactory or not. I have not seen the Genl myself yet. From what I can hear he is trying to make something big out of it, and nothing less than placing me in arrest and a trial before a court-martial will satisfy him; still I feel that any court will justify my leave and shall give myself no uneasiness about it.

Camp near Columbia, S. C.,
Feb. 5/65

Ere this reaches you, doubtless you will have heard that our army was driven from Broxton Bridge on Friday evening or Saturday, and had fallen back on Branchville, [S. C.]. The reports of the fight are very conflicting. Our loss is said to be heavy. The latest report yesterday evening, in town, was that the enemy were within eight miles of the railroad,[168] between Midway and Blackville;[169] the road may be cut ere this.

Camp near Columbia,
Feb. 10th, 1865

In Winnsboro[170] I met with Dr Ott, who said that the enemy had been repulsed at the bridge across the Edisto on Wednesday, but that the fighting was going on there again on Thursday, when he left; that the government stores were being sent off, in case the place should have to be evacuated. From

191

what I learned from him and Lieut Bell, of Capt A's company, our forces have burned the railbridge at Branchville, also the wagon bridge; that we have a few pickets at the different crossings on the Saltketchee[171] River; that they have burned Jackson Kearse's house, also the Cooner house. What other damage they have done I have not been able to learn. I hardly think they have been down as far as my house yet, unless they have done so in the last day or two.

It seems that the enemy are trying to make from Blackville across to Orangeburg C.[ourt] H.[ouse]. I will write again as soon as Capt A. returns, if I learn anything different.

Camp near Columbia, S. C.
Feb. 12th, 1865

We have had two false alarms here since my return & we had the command out nearly all night. The enemy were reported as burning a mill 16 miles from here yesterday morning & we sent out a scouting party to investigate the facts of the case, which proved to be false. Last night some of Whislin's stragling Cav. caused another false alarm & the whole command was ordered out; however, I was not among them as Genl Butler returned my explanation, that charges must be preferred against me for overstaying my leave. Therefore, I consider myself under arrest. Col R– went to see Genl B– this morning to ask him to release me & to accept of my explanation. But he told him he could not, that he only ordered the charges preferred for the sake of discipline & that he would be glad for me to call him (Genl B–) in as a witness in my behalf, that he would take great pleasure in testifying to my gallantry, punctuality, promptness in discharge of duty etc. There is no dishonor . . . to be court martialed for such an offense; besides I see & appreciate Genl B–['s] motive and I fully believe that the court will honorably acquit me. . . . [I]t may be the means of saving my life. Still, I regret being deferred the privilege of doing what I can in the defence of my native state which needs every son in her defence.

The enemy cut the R.R. at Orangeburg at 5 o'clock P. M. yesterday. Columbia may be their next aim, but I do not think so. My opinion is that they will turn their attention to Augusta or Charleston, most probably the former.

The people are fleeing from this place to N. C. There is a good deal of excitement around the city I understand. Genl Beauregard I understand is to assume command. I hope Sherman will soon come to grief. Our forces are too far scattered. I hope they will now be concentrated.

Camp near Columbia,<br>
Feb. 15, 1865

The enemy is in about eight miles of this place, on Congaree Creek, on the south side of the Congaree River. Some skirmishing occurred yesterday, and was kept up nearly all the evening. We are holding them in check and have a pretty good force in their front, and we are in hope that we will be able to repulse them at this point. I think I hear skirmishing going on now, but have not heard from the front this morning.

There is much excitement in the city, and the people are leaving in every direction, such moving of cattle, hogs, sheep, etc. I never saw the like before, nor never want to see again.

I was released temporarily from arrest on yesterday, ordered to report at Genl Butler's headquarters for orders, (I thought they could not do without me when a fight was going on). I reported and was ordered to establish a picket line on our left, extending to near the Saluda River; but as soon as I was ready to go, the order was countermanded, as Col Aiken was ordered over there with the whole command, and I got [the] chance to get the protection of my tent again last night, which was a source of great comfort. I have not been ordered to resume my arrest, but do not know when I will be ordered to, or what duty I will be called on to perform. I am looking for some order every minute. I expect a big fight will come off either today or tomorrow.

This place is but little fortified, and it will be open fight[ing] pretty much.

I hear pretty heavy skirmishing going on now below, on the creek.

Our Regiment is about eight miles from here. I am in

command of the whole Brigade camp, and tired of it, and want to be ordered to the front to take command of my regiment. Col R– is off moving his family to Lancaster, S. C.

Charlotte, N. C.,
Feb. 24th, 1865

I have heard that the enemy have passed through you all, but hope they have not destroyed everything. The enemy are moving in the direction of Wilmington, N. C.[172]
The cars ran as far as Blackstocks yesterday.

Charlotte, N. C.,
Feb. 27th/65

We are here awaiting orders. I do not know what the enemy are doing just now; have not heard anything of their movement in a day or two, though I believe they are moving in the direction of Wilmington, N. C. The cars ran as far as Blackstocks yesterday. . . . I heard from Ted Jack that my house & D's was burned.[173]

Charlotte, N. C.,
March 2nd, 1865

Our division has gone around in [the] rear of Sherman, and I understand is away down below Camden, on Lynch's creek; had captured some seven or eight wagons and teams. I expect to join them as soon as I can hear from Genl Butler, as Genl Lee has issued an order of amnesty[174] to all who have overstayed their time and who returned within twenty days from the 11th of Feb.

I would prefer going before a general court-martial, which, I believe, would acquit me honorably; but the campaign will be very active for a long while, and I will probably be deprived of my command for a long while. So I have concluded to demand my release, under Genl Lee's order.

Sherman's future movements are still a mystery; there is every probability of his passing around this place, whether he goes to Wilmington or not. Danville, I suppose, is his objective point.

Charlotte, N.C.,
March 4th, 1865

We move from here tomorrow in the direction of Salisbury and Greensboro, and I think in a short time we will be up as far as Raleigh, N. C. I understand we may go to Smithfield, near Goldsboro, N. C.

Charlotte, N. C.,
March 5th/65

I wrote you yesterday that we expect to leave today, but my information was not correct. We will doubtless leave in a day or two soon, possibly tomorrow.

Thomasville, N. C.,
March 11th, 1865

We are on the way to Raleigh, and were going by the way of Asheboro and Pittsboro, but the bridges on that route were destroyed; so we will go 'round on the road along the railroad. I expect we will be some seven or eight days yet in getting there, as the roads are awful.

I expect to resume my command as soon as we get up with the division, which I hope to meet near Raleigh.

We have had a rough time with the wagons; it has been rain, rain, all the time, and I know those at the front have had much worse.

I suppose you have heard of the death of Col Aiken, who was killed by a party of yankees in ambush in Marlboro District about twelve days ago.

I can give you no correct information from Sherman, except he is reported at Fayetteville, N. C.

Raleigh, N. C.,
March 21st, 1865

Col R. has gone back to South Carolina to gather up the desertions from the Brigade, about half of which have strayed or run away and gone back to the State; a sad state of affairs at this juncture.

Our Brigade has suffered very much since they left Columbia; not a great many have been killed, but a large number have been wounded, and a few captured.

Genl H. and staff and couriers, charged a party of yankees thribble[175] their number in Fayetteville the other day, and Genl H. led the party and killed one yankee with his sabre, another with his pistol, and captured a third himself, besides what the staff and others did, and put the rest to flight.

Genl Hardee[176] had an engagement with Sherman on last Saturday and Sunday, and captured, killed and wounded some thirty-five hundred, and only lost some four hundred, so says the paper; it is certain they were fighting.

Everything that is mounted has gone to the front, about thirty-five miles from here.

Raleigh, N. C.,
March 23rd, 1865

I have just received an order releasing me from arrest, and I will leave early tomorrow morning for the front.

I understand that Genl Johnston continues to whip Sherman; but from what I can gather, our army has withdrawn back to Smithfield, some eight or ten miles, on account of the very bad roads, and to take up a much better position; that he only fought them at Bentonville, where he whipped them, last week in order to give him more time.

*After Colonel Stokes' release had come through, there was little time remaining in the war; the Regiment was approximately eighty-five percent under strength. There was nothing left for him to salvage except that which could never be taken away: honor.*

Camp, Logan's Brigade,
Wayne County, N. C.,
March 29th, 1865

We have only moved about six miles since I wrote you on last Monday, and I hope are likely to remain here for several days still, to recruit up the command and get everything cleaned up,

196

etc. We are now encamped on the Raleigh and Goldsboro road, not far from the railroad,[177] on the west side of Little River. The Regiment was in bad condition sure enough; still the others in the Brigade were not a great deal better. I have been exerting myself and hope soon to have it up to the proper standard. We have about one hundred fifteen present for duty mounted, exclusive of officers, and a good many others in the dismounted battalion. But I am sorry to say, that I believed the larger portion of the Regiment is in S. C., in fact of the whole Brigade is there.

Hoats, from Capt A's company, and four men of the 5th S. C. Cavalry, from Colleton District, deserted a few nights ago and went back to S. C., carrying arms and everything with them. I expect they think they will be safe down there now. It is too bad for our soldiers to be doing so at this time, and examples ought to be made of some of them, and I think will.

I hear that Genl Young[178] had a fight with the yankees near Branchville, S. C. a few days ago, and one report says they whipped him and another says he whipped them badly. That he had a fight there seems to be a certainty, and I am afraid it occurred about the time Doctor got down there with my mules and that they might have been captured. I am afraid that Doctor has done bad business by going back; and although you could not well have denied him the use of the mules, there being so little civil law existing now, I suppose, in the lower part of the State, (below Columbia, I suppose) and so many lawless soldiers, that he ought to have gotten a white man to go along with him to bring them back and not have trusted it to a negro boy, such as Morgan.

Our wagon train is up with the command now.

This has been announced in orders as Logan's[179] Brigade.

### Wednesday evening.

The command has just been ordered to saddle up and be in readiness. The enemy are reported advancing.

Camp, Logan's Brigade,
Wayne County, N. C.,
April 1st, 1865

Capt Appleby has not arrived yet, though the letter you sent by him reached me this morning. I understand Col R. has detained him to assist in gathering up the men, or in doing nothing, as is generally believed they will all do, here by those in higher authority. Capt A is absent without leave, and will be marked so, and will certainly get himself into trouble unless Col R. can clear him; and Genl L.[ogan] says he has no authority to detain him.

That was only a small foraging party that disturbed our quiet the other day. We did not go out of camp; and the foraging party made another dash into the pickets of the 1st South Carolina Cavalry yesterday, but all was soon quiet again. How long our quiet will remain I cannot say, but hope for some days yet.

The camp report is that the regiments of the Brigade are to go back to South Carolina, one at a time, to gather up their men and return in thirty days, and that the 5th Regiment is to leave in a few days. There may be some truth in it, but I do not care for my regiment to go at all for only thirty days.

Arrangements are being made to furlough those men who have stuck to the command from Columbia and those who have never been home since they left last spring.

Apr 2nd

P. S.—I had a very fine shad for breakfast this morning, given me by Col Davis, who sent some men out seining in the Neuse [River] yesterday.

*Extract from Records of Individual Service*

On April 10th, Sherman commenced to move from Goldsboro up through North Carolina along the Central railroad, and the command skirmished daily with his advance until we passed through Raleigh, on Saturday, the 15th of April, when near Hillsboro a flag of truce came up from the enemy, which

I met.  It was the beginning of negotiations  between Generals Johnstone[180] and Sherman, which eventually ended in the surrender of Johnstone's Army.

Hearing on the evening of the 26th of April that the surrender would take place the following day, and not desiring to go through the formality of surrendering the Regiment which I commanded, I ordered the camp struck at 8:30 P. M. and marched toward Asheboro, N. C.  Reached Asheboro at 8:30 P. M. April 27th.  At this place I disbanded the Regiment and sent them home.

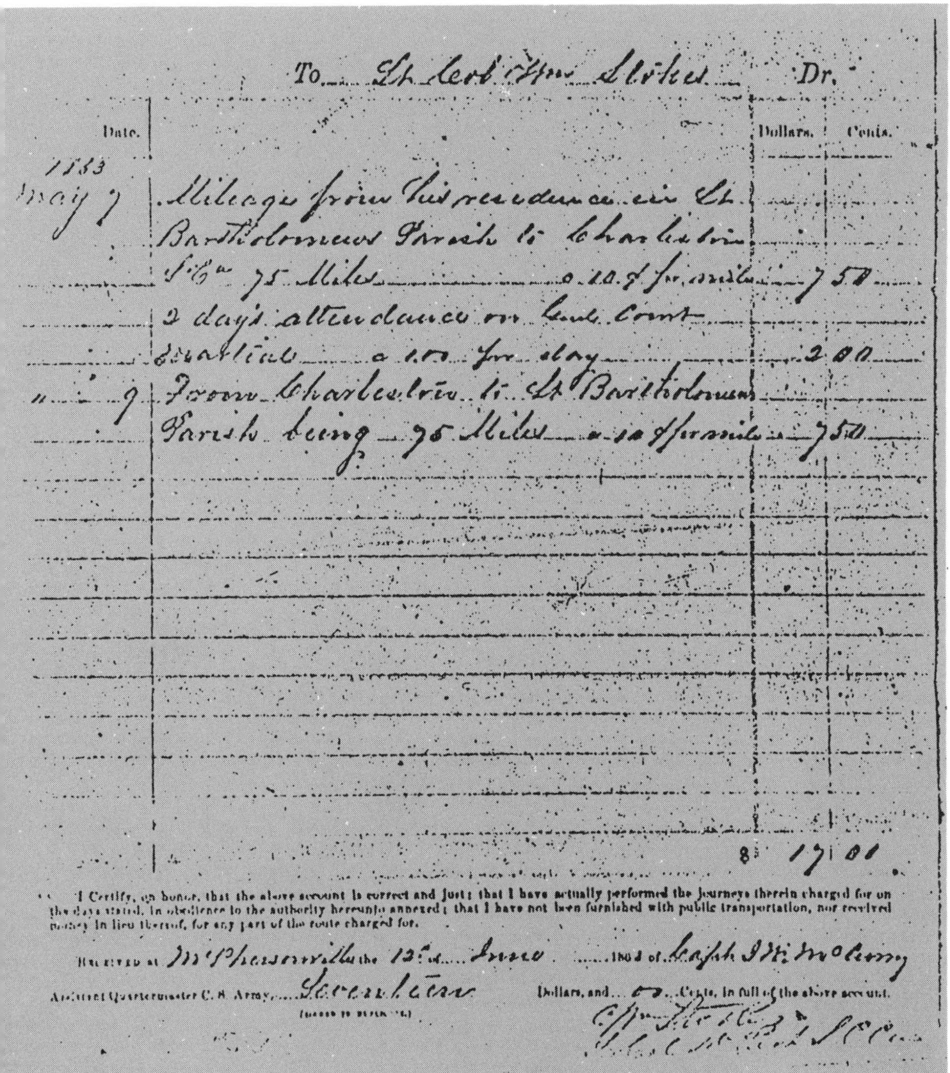

**Confederate States of America,**

WAR DEPARTMENT,

Richmond, *April 2nd* 1864

You are hereby informed that the President has appointed you

*Lieutenant Colonel*

*4th South Carolina Cav'y Reg't*

In the Provisional Army in the service of the Confederate States: to rank as such from the *Sixteenth* day of *December* one thousand eight hundred and sixty *two*. Should the Senate, at their next session, advise and consent thereto, you will be commissioned accordingly.

Immediately on receipt hereof, please to communicate to this Department, through the Adjutant and Inspector General's Office, your acceptance or non-acceptance of said appointment; and with your letter of acceptance, return to the Adjutant and Inspector General the OATH, herewith enclosed, properly filled up, SUBSCRIBED and ATTESTED, reporting at the same time your AGE, RESIDENCE when appointed, and the STATE in which you were BORN.

Should you accept, you will report for duty to *Col Rutledge*

*James A. Seddon*

Secretary of War.

*Lieut Col Wm Stokes*
*4th S C Cavalry*
*P. A. C. S.*

# BARNWELL
# DISTRICT TROOP.

A few more men are wanted for this Troop.

The pay is Twenty-Three Dollars per month.

Men of means are entreated to give us the use of (each one) a horse, to mount such volunteers as are unable to mount themselves. A large number have already contributed. Other Districts have done the same. Come forward, like men, and save the honor of the District.

**JOHN E. TOBIN.**

Blackville, August 23, 1861.

**(Confederate.)**

**10 Batt'n Cavalry.** | **S. C.**

*Wm Stokes* ×

*Major*, 2 Batt'n Cav., South Carolina Vols.*

Appears on

**Field and Staff Muster Roll**

of the organization named above,

for *July & Aug.* , 186_2_

Date of Commission, or }
Regimental Appointment. } ———— 186

Station ————————————

Present or absent *Not stated*

Remarks: ————————————
————————————————
————————————————
————————————————
————————————————

× *Signs Certificate as Inspector*
*& Mustering Officer*

*This battalion was organized in January, 1862, and officially designated by the A. & I. G. O. as the 3d Battalion South Carolina Cavalry, but it was mustered in the field as the 2d Battalion South Carolina Cavalry. In September, 1862, the official designation was changed to the 10th Battalion South Carolina Cavalry.
By S. O. No. 224, Headquarters Department of South Carolina, Georgia and Florida, dated December 16, 1862, this battalion was consolidated with the 12th Battalion South Carolina Cavalry and two independent companies and formed the 4th Regiment South Carolina Cavalry.*

Book mark: ————————————

*W. Fennel*

(84501) Copyist.

---

**(Confederate.)**

**10 Batt'n Cavalry.** | **S. C.**

*William Stokes*

*Major*, 2 Batt'n Cav., South Carolina Vols.*

Appears on

**Field and Staff Muster Roll**

of the organization named above,

for *Sept. & Oct.* , 186_2_

Date of Commission, or } *May 6* , 186_2_
Regimental Appointment. }

Station *Camp Pritchard*

Present or absent *Absent*

Remarks: *1st Major Wm Stokes*
*absent for 30 days on sick*
*furlough on account of hemor-*
*rhage of the Lungs*
————————————————
————————————————
————————————————

*This battalion was organized in January, 1862, and officially designated by the A. & I. G. O. as the 3d Battalion South Carolina Cavalry, but it was mustered in the field as the 2d Battalion South Carolina Cavalry. In September, 1862, the official designation was changed to the 10th Battalion South Carolina Cavalry.
By S. O. No. 224, Headquarters Department of South Carolina, Georgia and Florida, dated December 16, 1862, this battalion was consolidated with the 12th Battalion South Carolina Cavalry and two independent companies and formed the 4th Regiment South Carolina Cavalry.*

Book mark: ————————————

*W. Fennel*

(84501) Copyist.

# APPENDIX I: 5

Hd Qrs Detachment Rutledge
Cav. S. C. V. Camp Prichard (sic)
Dec. 19th, 1862

Brig Genl Thos Jordan:
                    Chief of Staff & A.A.Genl

Sir:

        I would respectfully beg leave
to call the attention of the Genl.
Commanding to a mistake that
occurred in my name as Lt Col
of Rutledge Cav. S. C. V. in being
designated as W. E. Stokes, when
it is simply Wm Stokes.  I hope it
will be corrected, as there is a
W. E. Stokes, who is not in the army.

                    Very respectfully
                    your obt. servt.,
                    /s/ Wm Stokes
                    Lt Col Comd'g


Respectfully forwarded)
This: Brig Genl. Walker)

205

(Confederate.)

| 1 | 4 Cav. | S.C. |

_Wm Stokes_

_1st Lt._, Co. ___, 4 Reg't South Carolina Cav.

Appears on a

Roster

of the organization named above.

Roster dated

_Not dated_, 186 .

Appointed _Dec 16_, 1863.

Remarks :

The 4th (also known as Rutledge's) Regiment South Carolina Cavalry was formed by the consolidation of the 10th and
14th Battalions South Carolina Cavalry and Captains Pinckney's and Rutledge's Independent Companies, South Carolina
Cavalry, by S. O. No. 254, Hdqrs. Dept. S. C., Ga. and Fla.,
dated December 16, 1862.

Book mark :

_(9) Williams_

(443) Copyist.

---

(CONFEDERATE.)

_S 1 4 Cav SC_
_Wm Stokes_
_Lt Col PACS_

Appears on a

Register

of Appointments, Confederate States Army.

State _S Carolina_
To whom report _4 S C Cav Regt_
Date of appointment _April 2_, 1864
Date of confirmation _June 10_, 1864
To take rank _Decem 16_, 1862
Date of acceptance _May 6_, 1864
Delivered _Dept S C, Ga, & Fla_
Subsequent disposition
Secretary of War _J. A. Seddon_
Remarks _Appointed under_
_Constitutional authority_
_vested in the President._

Confed. Arch., Chap. 1, File No. 93, page 328

_Q. F. Taylor_

(C79) Copyist.

Hd Qurs 3d Mily Dist SC
McPhersonville Sept 20. 1863.

Lieut Col W Stokes, 4th SCC
    Commdg at Crew Pond.
        Colonel:

            The Brig Genl Commdg directs
me to apprise you of the pleasure it affords him
to forward to you the following copy of a letter
recevd on yesterday from Dept Hd Qurs in the
expresions of which he heartily Concurs.

                Hd Qurs Dept SC Ga & Fla
                Charleston SC Sept 19. 1863.

    General:

            The Commdg General has read the report
of Col Stokes, and he desires you to express to that
Officer his sense of the untiring energy and skill
which resulted in the Capture of a portion of the telegraph party of the enemy.

            He also instructed me to call your attention
to the reprehensible Conduct of certain pickets of
the 11th SC Regt, by whose negligence eleven of the
enemy were allowed to pass without being either
halted or fired on, and their subsequent misbe-
haviour.        You will please have this matter investigated, to the end that proper punishment may be inflicted on the derelict par-

```
                              Hd Quars Mity Dist SC
                              McPhersonville  Sept 20.1863

Lieut Col  W Stokes. 4th SCC
        Cmmdg at Green Pond

        Colonel:
                    The Brig Gen Commdg directs
me to aprise [sic] you of the pleasure it affords him
to forward to you the following copy of a letter
received on yesterday from Dept Hd Qrs. in the
expressions of which he heartily concurs.

                        Hd Qrs Dept SC Ga & Fla
                          Charleston SC. Sept 19. 1863

General:

        The Cmmdg General has read the report
of Col Stokes, and he desires you to express to that
Officer his sense of the untiring energy and skill
which resulted in the capture of a portion of the tele-
graph party of the enemy.
        He also instructed me to call your attention
to the reprehensible conduct of certain pickets of
the 11th SC Regt, by whose negligence eleven of the
enemy were allowed to pass without being either
halted or fired on and their subsequent misbe-
haviour.  You will please have this matter
ter investigated to the end that proper pun-
ishment may be inflicted on the derelict par-
ties.
        Respectfully
                Your obedient servant
            (Sgd)    Clifton H Smith
                        AAGenl

Brig Gen W S Walker
  Hd Military District
                        Very respectfully
                            Your obedient servant
                        /s/James Ward Asst AG
```

```
                          Poctaligo [sic] Dec 20th, 1863
Brig Genl Thos Jordan
         Chief of Staff.

                       Genl:

                              I respectfully
ask a leave of absence for twelve
days to go to the upper part of
this state to make arrange-
ments for accuiring [sic] my ne-
groes.

              Very respecfully [sic]
                 your oby. servt.,
                 /s/ Wm Stokes
                    Lt Col 4th S. C. Cav.
```

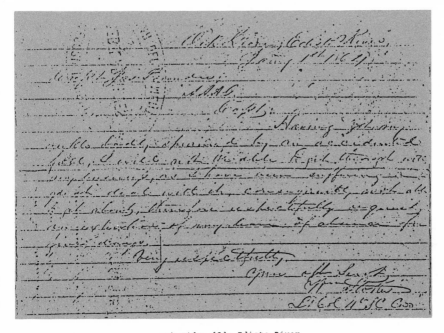

Oak Ridge [?]; Edisto River,
Jany. 1st 1864
Capt Jas. Loundec [?]:
A.A.A.G.
Capt:
Having got my
ankle badly sprained by an accidental
fall, I will not be able to get through with
my business, as I have been suffering a
great deal with it, consequently not able
to get about, therefore respectfully request
an extension of my leave of absence for
five days.
Very respectfully,
your obt. servt.,
/s/ Wm Stokes
Lt Col 4th S. C. Cav.

Charleston Decemr 16th 1863.

Liut Col: C. W. Stokes
Captain John C Calhoun
Captain W. P. Appleby
    Committee
        Green Pond So. Ca.
            Gentlemen
                Your letter of 11th was
received by us this morning. —
    We cannot reply to your enquiries, as to the
balance that may be due for cost of a sword ordered by Capt. Courtenay (our books being in
Columbia). Nor can we give an explanation, touch-
ing the presentation of the sword by Capt. Trenholm
as referred to by Major Willis— We shall therefore forward your letter to our house in Columbia
where it will receive the attention of our Mr G. A
Trenholm who will reply to it. —
        Very Respectfully
            Jno. Fraser & Co

We address this letter
as requested to
        Captn Jno C Calhoun
            Pocotaligo
                So Ca.

1091.

**Office Confederate States General Purchasing Agent and Sup't R. R. Transportation,**
DEPARTMENT OF SOUTH CAROLINA, GEORGIA AND FLORIDA.

Charleston, S. C. 16th Nov. 1863.

Lt. Col. W. Stokes.

Gentlemen. I've answered letters enough about this forage matter, & I think very strange that I am first catechised by Capt Courtenay & then by you; as if I had committed some misdemeanor — when all that I've done was for Capt Winder. — I never knew you in connection with the forage until a few days ago & all I've to say I am quite tired of it, I've assumed this much, & I will do no more & I care very little about it myself — for it now became very annoying — I told him to present the forage to whom he pleased in the name of whomever he pleased. All I wanted was if it was not presented by Capt Lewis=holm that it should be paid for — to the parties that sent it to me —

I am with most respect [illegible]

Head Quars Dept S.C. Ga & Fla
Charleston Dec 18th 1863

General Order
No. 128.

II. The illegal impressment of any description of private property is forbidden within the limits of this Department, and it is especially enjoined on all Commanding Officers to suppress or prevent it. When private property is thus forcibly taken without the strictest conformity to law regulations and the orders of the War Department, it can only be regarded as a licentious use of power, and actually robbery under the Cloak of Authority. An Officer or Agent guilty of it will be held accountable if reported for his misconduct.

By Command of Genl Beauregard

Sigd. Thomas Jordan
Chief of Staff

Head Quars   Dep.t   S.C.   Ga & Fla

Charleston   Dec 18th   1863

General Order
    No 1218.

II. The illegal impressment
of any description of private property is forbidden within the limits of this Department,
and it is specially enjoined on all Commanding Officers to suppress or prevent it when
private property is thus forciably taken without
the strictest conformity to law regulations
and the orders of the War Department, it
can only be regarded as licentious use of
power and actually robbery under the cloak
of authority.  An Officer or Agent guilty
of it will be held accountable if reported
for his misconduct.

By Command of Genl Beauregard

Signed                        Thomas Jordan

Chief of Staff

215

# APPENDIX I: 13

Post Qr Mr Office
Hardeeville SC
April 5/64

My Dear Colonel

As you are about to leave for Va with your Regiment, I cannot let the opportunity pass, of making my acknowledg-ments to you, for your uniform Courtesy, during a Service of nearly two years on the Coast & for a portion of this time in close official intercourse—

You have been engaged in an arduous Service & without notice, I may say, from the Country—but you have discha your duty well & those who have been near you, will always take pleasure in saying so.

Upon your new field of duty—you have my best wishes for your Success & Safety—

with the assurance of my Regard

I am your obt servt

Wm A Courtenay
Capt &c

Lt Col Wm Stokes
4th SC Cav

[Envelope: Miss ___ ___
Cranchville
S.C.] Stony Creek Station
June 30th 1864

Dear Aunt

Col. Stoke requested
me to say to you (as he did not have
time himself) that he was ordered
to the reserve Camp, twenty or miles
above Richmond, to bring up the
oxen & horses from that place
& perhaps you would not hear
from him in a week or more
as it will take him at least that
long to get to us. We are still burying
in the yanks by the hundreds. J.M.
Liston is gone with the Col. till
his wife. We are having lively
here. We rout the Yanks on every
occasion, but have to fight hard
for it. We scatter them like sheep
any time is that. Tell Mother &
am well. R. Risher is well. When
you write again, direct your letter
to Stony Creek Station Va,

217

Tell Dr. Stokes, the Yankee Cavalry Cant Stand Butlers Brigade. They give up almost as Soon as they find out who they are fighting. Just let them know that Butlers Brigade is along & the battle is half fought. but I am sorry to say that our horses are almost played out & It would not be amiss to say our men & horses for we have been going day & night. I have now for duty eight men. What a large command for a Captain! Give my love to all

Yours &c

W. Y. Appleby

P.S. Tell the Dr I will write to him when I get time, tell him to write to me. Tell Sarah & Robert & all you See to direct their letters as I have told you above—

Stony Creek Station

June 30th 1864

Dear Aunt

Col. Stokes requested
me to say to you (as he did not have
time himself) that he was ordered
to the reserve Camp, twenty miles
above Richmond, to bring us the
men & horses from that place
& perhaps you would not hear
from him in a week or more
as it will take him at least that
long to get to us. We are still bringing
in the yanks by the hundreds. I. M.
Liston is gone with the Col. Tell
his wife. We are having lively times
hear [sic]. We route the yanks on every
occasion, but have to fight hard
for it. We scatter them like sheep.
My time is short. Tell Mother I
am well. R. Risher is well. When
you write again, direct your letter
to Stony Creek Station Va.
Tell Dr. Stokes, the yankee
Cavalry cant [sic] stand Butler's
Brigade. They give up almost as
soon as they find out who they

are fighting.  Just let them know

that Butler's Brigade is along &

the battle is half fought, but I

am sorry to say that our horses are

almost played out & it would

not be amiss to say men &

horses for we have been going day

& night.  I have now for duty eight

men.  What a large command for

a Captain.  Give my love to all

Yours &

/s/Wm Appleby


P.S.  Tell the Dr. I will write

to him when I get time.  Tell him

to write to me.  Tell Sarah Rish-

er & all you see to direct their

letters as I have told you above.

| (CONFEDERATE.) | (CONFEDERATE.) |
|---|---|
| S. 1 4 Cav. S.C. | S. 1 4 Cav. S.C. |
| W. Stoakes* | William Stokes |
| Lt. Col. 4 Regt. S.C. Cav. | Lt. Col. 4 Regt. S.C. Cav. |

*(left card)*

Appears on a

Report of Sick and Wounded

in
General Hospital,
at
Huguenot Springs, Va.,

for the week ending _July 7_, 1864.

Remarks: _Received into Hospital_

Book mark: _____

_T. Cay_

(040)

Copyist.

*(right card)*

Appears on a

Register

containing Rosters of Commissioned Officers, Provisional Army Confederate States.

Date of appointment ___Dec 16___, 1862

Date of resignation, death, transfer or promotion } _____ , 186 .

Remarks : _____

Confed. Arch., Chap. 1, File No. 81, page 512

_M. C. Lemerd_

(055)

Copyist.

*[notice the name has been misspelled]

(FEDERATE.)

1 | 4 Cav | S.C.

Wm Stokes

Lt Col. 4 Regt S.C. Cav

Appears on a

Register

containing Rosters of Commissioned Officers, Provisional Army Confederate States.

Remarks: ...................................................

Confed. Arch., Chap. 1, File No. 96, page *144*

W L Ray
Copyist.

(645)

(CONFEDERATE.)

8 | 4 Cav. | S.C.

W. Stoakes *

Lt. Col. 4 Regt. S.C. Cav.

Appears on a

Report of Sick and Wounded

in          General Hospital,

at          Huguenot Springs, Va.,

for the week ending *July 14* ,  186 *4*

Remarks: *Retd to duty*.

Book mark: .................................................

J. Cary
Copyist.

(645)

*[notice the name has been misspelled]

No. 17.

(CONFEDERATE.)

J | 4 Cav | S. C.

*Wm Stokes*

*Lt Col 4 Regt S.C.C.*

Appears on an

### Inspection Report

of Butler's Cavalry Brigade, commanded by Col.
B. H. Rutledge,

Report dated *near Hicksford*
*Va Dec 31* 1864.

Date of muster of organ- }
    ization into service } _____, 186_.

Term of service _____

Absent commissioned officers accounted for:

By what authority *Furlough 21 days*
*from Dec 23/64 Gen Lee*

Date _____ *Dec 23*, 1864

Remarks : _____

_____

Inspection Report P., No. 43; inclosure 6.

*A S Douglas*
Copyist.

(654)

4111'

---

(Confederate.)

4 Cav. | S. C.

*Wm Stokes*
*Lt Col* 4 Reg't South Carolina Cavalry.

Appears on

### Field and Staff Muster Roll

of the organization named above,

for *Sept + Oct*, 1864.

Date of Commission, or }  *Dec 16*, 1862
Regimental Appointment, }

Station _____

Present or absent *Present*

Remarks : _____

_____

_____

_____

_____

_____

Enrolled or Enlisted the Regt

The 4th (also known as Rutledge's) Regiment South Carolina Cavalry was formed by the consolidation of the 10th and
12th Battalions South Carolina Cavalry and Captains Pinckney's and Rutledge's Independent Companies, South Carolina
Cavalry, by S. O. No. 294, Hdqrs. Dept. S. C., Ga. and Fla.,
dated December 16, 1862.

Book mark : _____

*T M William*
Copyist.

(632)

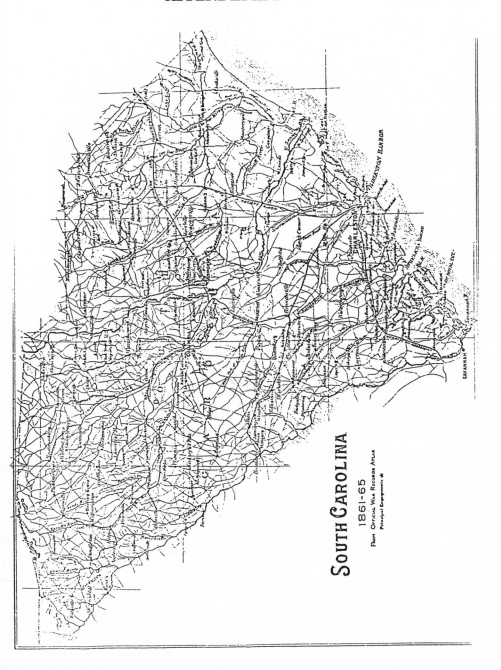

South Carolina
1861-65
From Official War Records Atlas
Principal Engagements ★

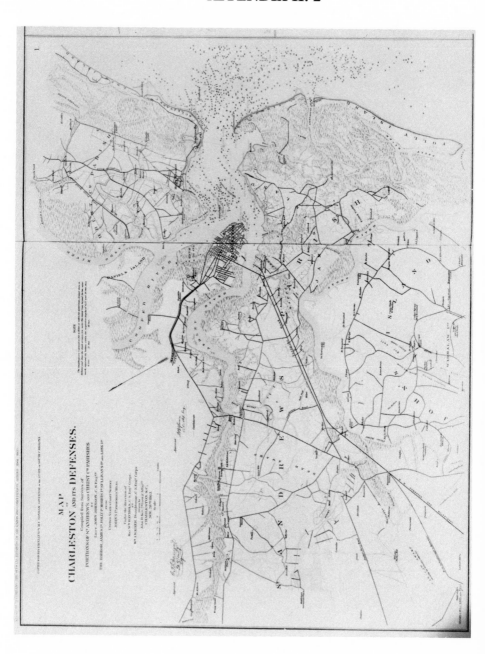

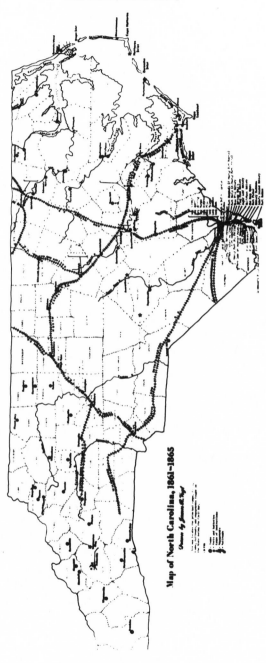

Map of North Carolina, 1861–1865

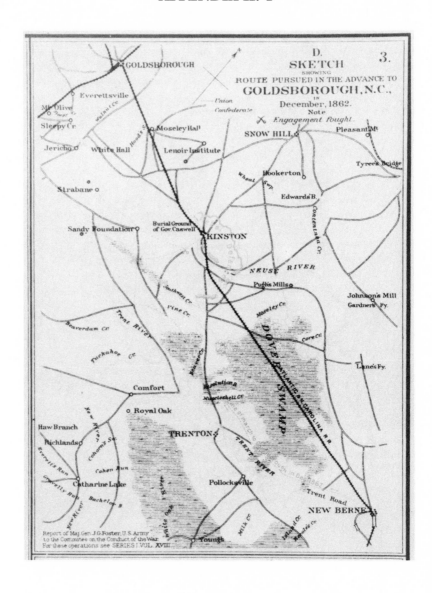

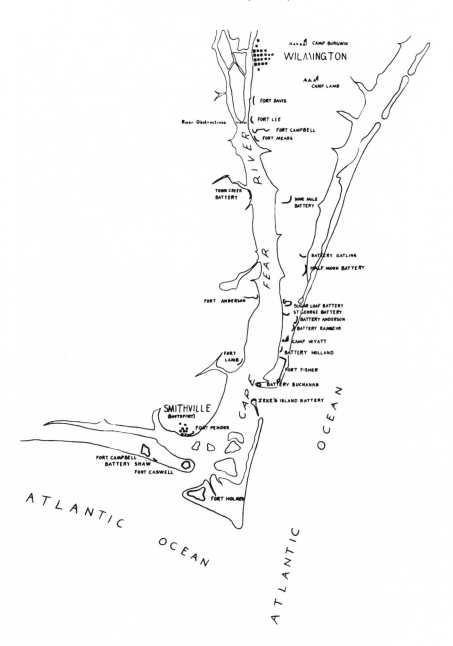

229

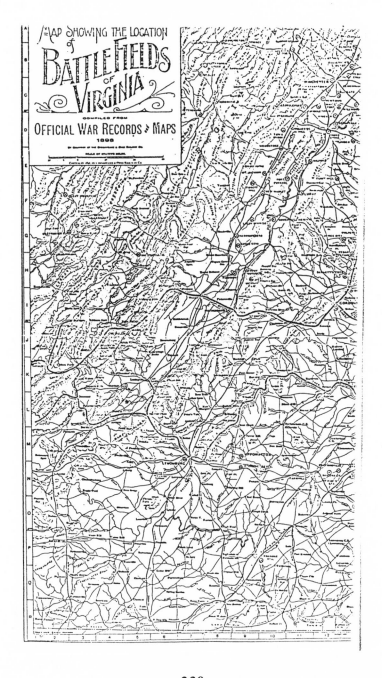

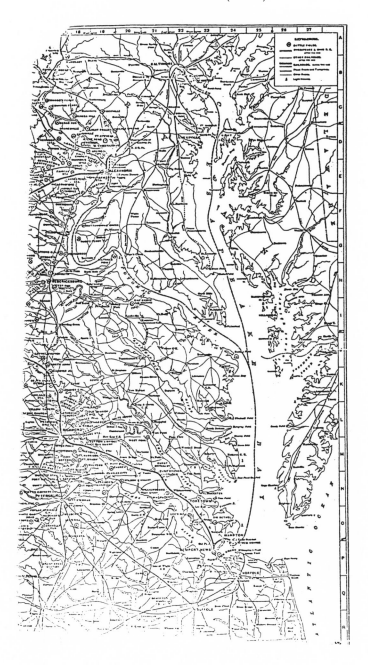

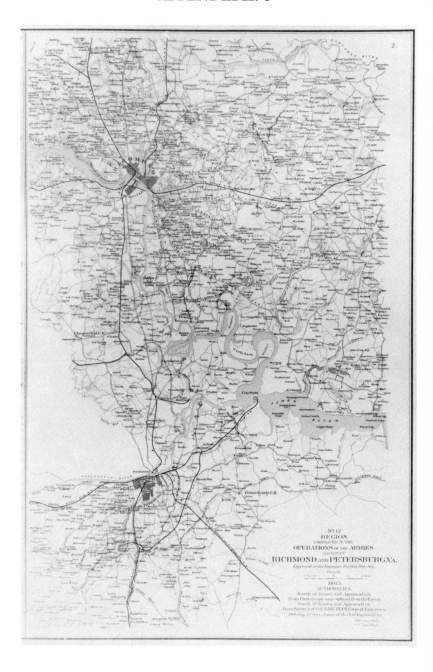

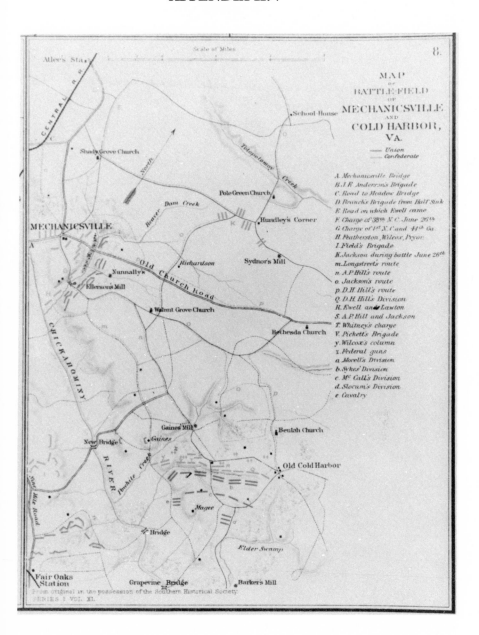

MAP
OF
BATTLE-FIELD
OF
MECHANICSVILLE
AND
COLD HARBOR,
VA.
Union
Confederate

A. *Mechanicsville Bridge*
B. *J.R.Anderson's Brigade*
C. *Road to Meadow Bridge*
D. *Branch's Brigade from Half Sink*
E. *Road on which Ewell came*
F. *Charge of 38th N.C. June 26th*
G. *Charge of 1st N.C. and 44th Ga.*
H. *Featherston, Wilcox, Pryor.*
I. *Field's Brigade*
K. *Jackson during battle June 26th*
m. *Longstreet's route*
n. *A.P.Hill's route*
o. *Jackson's route*
p. *D.H. Hill's route*
Q. *D.H. Hill's Division*
R. *Ewell and Lawton*
S. *A.P.Hill and Jackson*
T. *Whitney's charge*
V. *Pickett's Brigade*
y. *Wilcox's column*
z. *Federal guns*
a. *Morell's Division*
b. *Sykes' Division*
c. *Mc Call's Division*
d. *Slocum's Division*
e. *Cavalry*

1091.                              [12 July 1862]

Hd. Qrs. McPhersonville 3d Dist.
            July 12th

Maj. Wm Stokes.

    Maj.

        I desire you to have
placed in readiness at some se-
                                    Landing
cure point convenient to Boyd's in a
                        with the oars
large row boat, and a canoe
that will hold three men.
    Have it done at the earliest
practicable moment, as they
will be required for immediate use,
perhaps to-night.
    Also send some one with a
flag to reconnoitre whether any
men of the enemy can be seen on
Port Royal Island.

                    Very respectfully
                        W S Walker
                        Col. Comdg

Hd. Qrs. McPhersonville July 13th

Maj. Wm Stokes

Major:

Upon information obtained yesterday in regard to the enemy I expected to have used the boat and canoe last night. In the afternoon however, matters had changed, which prevented the immediate use. They may be required however soon.

Very respectfully,
yr. obdt. Servt.

W L Walker
Col. Comdg.

Hd Qr. 5th Mil. Dist.
McPhersonville S.C.
July 20th

Maj. Wm Stokes
Comdg. 2d Battal. Cavy,
Maj.

Capt. Stephen Elliott,
will go to Grahamville To-morrow morning
for the purpose of making a boat expedition
against the enemy's pickets. He will
take a four pounder to be placed in one of
the boats. He take men enough with
him To man one boat. I desire you to
furnish men enough to man another
to accompany him. Two boats will be
allowed to accompany him, if you find it
expedient. The whole force to be under
his command.

very respectfully,
yr. obt. servt.
W. Walker
Col. Comdg.

P.S. I would call your attention
to some extracts from a Yankee
letter from Hilton Head as very probably indi-
-cating the plans of the enemy in operations along
the coast — in Mercury of 17th inst. W.W.

238

# NOTES

1.    This company was successively designated as the Hammond Hussars; Captain Stokes' Company, 2 Battalion Cavalry, South Carolina Volunteers; Company D and Company C, 2 Battalion S. C. Cavalry (organized in January 1862), and officially designated by the Adjutant and Inspector General's Office as the 3 Battalion S. C. Cavalry but was mustered in the field as the 2 Battalion S. C. Cavalry. In September 1862, the official designation was changed to the 10 Battalion S. C. Cavalry.

By S.O. No. 254, Headquarters Department of South Carolina, Georgia and Florida, dated December 16, 1862, this battalion was consolidated with the 12 Battalion S. C. Cavalry and two independent companies and formed the 4th Regiment S. C. Cavalry, C. S. A. General Stokes' original company was designated Company G of the regiment.

2.    The only clue to his residence is contained in a voucher reimbursing General Stokes for service on a court-martial at the rate of ten cents/mile and one dollar/day subsistence. See Appendix I, No. 1.

3.    See Appendix I, No. 2.

4.    The law demanded a prescribed period of time so that all who wished to run for the office could be afforded the opportunity to elect to do so. There was also a closing date ending the entry of any additional candidates.

5.    The officer who carried the colors in a troop of cavalry: the cornet of horse.

6.    General R. S. Ripley who, in the spring of 1863, would command from the South Santee to the Stono rivers and Rantowles Creek in preparation for the defense of Charleston and Savannah.

7.    Brigadier General Thomas Fenwick Drayton commanded the Fifth Military District under General R. E. Lee, and the Sixth and Fourth Districts under General Pemberton; his headquarters was at Hardeeville.

8.     Colonel (later, Brigadier General) John Smith Preston, served on the staff of General Beauregard in 1861 and 1862. At the end of the war, he was in charge of the Bureau of Conscription.

9.     Lieutenant General John Clifford Pemberton commanded the Department of South Carolina, Georgia and Florida in early 1862 as a major general.

10.    Major General Daniel S. Donelson of Tennessee, having commanded a brigade in West Virginia in 1861, was sent to Charleston in early 1862.

11.    Brigadier General Maxcy Gregg was promoted to this rank in December of 1861 and ordered to South Carolina, where he commanded a brigade composed of the First, Twelfth, Thirteenth, and Fourteenth Regiments.

12.    Pocotaligo.

13.    A vault or chamber, especially in a rampart, with embrasures for artillery.

14.    Flatboats.

15.    Hog's Neck.

16.    General Stokes has not been able to see his new son who was born on June 17, 1862.

17.    A newspaper.

18.    Beaufort.

19.    Bonus.

20.    This portion of the rumor was not accurate, as the designation of the unit became the 4th Regiment. See note 1.

21.    Pritchard.

22.    This is apparently in reference to Sergeant Major J. E. Williams, who died of typhoid fever on May 17, 1862.

23.    Corinth.

24.     This seems to be a power play, a threat: agree or lose a senior command position in the new regiment.

25.     The reference is obviously about a new regiment that will be formed (with Major Stokes' battalion included in it) and to the objections to Rutledge as the commanding officer.

26.     The collar insignia of rank for officers in the Army of the Confederacy was as follows:
Second Lieutenant – 1 horizontal bar.
First Lieutenant – 2 horizontal bars.
Captain – 3 horizontal bars.
Major – 1 five-pointed star.
Lt Colonel – 2 five-pointed stars.
Colonel – 3 five-pointed stars.
General – 3 five-pointed stars encircled by a wreath.

27.     Brigadier General States R. Gist, commander of the troops on James Island. He was killed in action on November 30, 1864, at the battle of Franklin, Tennessee.

28.     The reference is to the train.

29.     It was tailored when he gained promotion to major.

30.     Brigadier General Hugh W. Mercer was in command of Savannah during most of the war.

31.     The reference is to confirm his recovery from the severe lung problems for which he was hospitalized for a month in September and October.

32.     Rappahannock.

33.     The original order listed him as W. E. Stokes.  See Appendix I, No. 5.

34.     Captain W. P. DuBose, adjutant of the Holcombe Legion.

35.     General Pierre Gustave Toutant Beauregard had been assigned command of the Department of South Carolina, Georgia and Florida on August 29, 1862.

36.     Captain W. E. Earle.

37.     Captain Clark conducted the inspection on December 20, 1862.

38.     Refer to the incident in December 1862. Dr. Rivers was to be brought up on charges of being drunk on duty and misappropriation of hospital stores, i.e., whiskey. The charges were to be dropped in exchange for his resignation.

39.     James Alexander Seddon, 1815-1880, of Fredericksburg, Virginia., was Secretary of War from 1862 until 1865.

40.     Brigadier General W. S. Walker was assigned command of the Third Military District of South Carolina on May 28, 1862.

41.     On the Charleston and Savannah Railroad.

42.     The Confederate States had no actual navy at the beginning of the war. The South, however, managed to construct a fleet of ironclads during the next four years to equal any in the world including:

The *Merrimac*, of ten guns—two 7-inch Brooke rifles, two 6.4-inch Brooke rifles, six 9-inch Dahlgren smoothbores.
The *Louisiana*, of sixteen guns—Brooke rifles of 7- and 6.4-inch calibre, and 8- and 9-inch Dahlgren smoothbores.
The *Manassas*, a turtle-back ram—one 68-pounder, smoothbore.
The *Arkansas*, of ten guns—two 8-inch columbiads, four 6.4-inch rifles, two 9-inch Dahlgrens, and two 32-pounders, smoothbore.
The *Palmetto State*, of four guns—one 80-pounder rifle, one 60-pounder, and two 8-inch shell guns.
The *Chicora*, of four guns—two 32-pounders, rifled, and two 9-inch shell guns.
The *Richmond*, of four guns—one 7-inch Brooke rifle, two 6.4-inch Brooke rifles and one 10-inch smoothbore.
The *Virginia*, of four guns—one 7-inch Brooke rifle, two 6.4-inch Brooke rifles, and one 10-inch smoothbore.
The *Fredericksburg*, of four guns—two 6.4-inch Brooke rifles, one 11-inch smoothbore, and one 8-inch smoothbore.
The *Albemarle*, of two guns—two 7-inch Brooke rifles.

The *Atlanta*, of four guns—two 7-inch and two 6.4-inch Brooke rifles.

The *Tennessee*, of six guns—two 7-inch and four 6.4-inch Brooke rifles.

The *Savannah*, of four guns—probably two Brooke rifles and two smoothbores.

The *Columbia*, of eight guns—probably Brooke rifles and smoothbores.

The *Charleston*, of six guns—four Brooke rifles and two 9-inch Dahlgren shell guns.

The *North Carolina*, of four guns—probably two Brooke rifles and two smoothbores.

The *Raleigh*, of four guns—probably two Brooke rifles and two smoothbores.

The *Georgia*, of seven guns—smoothbores and rifles.

The *Milledgeville*, probably identical to the *Savannah*. (Not completed when burned to prevent capture.)

The *Neuse*, similar to the *Albemarle*, but burned to prevent capture.

The *Mississippi*, burned to prevent capture. Pronounced by the United States and Confederate States naval officers the most powerful vessel in the world.

The information above appears in Clement A. Evans' *Confederate Military History, XII.*

43.    The reference is to General Stokes' brother-in-law.

44.    The total forces of the Confederates in February 1863 numbered about 15,500 for the defense of South Carolina; by April, General Beauregard would command nearly 22,650. The combined Union forces, under the command of Major General David Hunter and Rear Admiral S. F. DuPont, were more than twice that number. With the war raging in Virginia and in the West, the resources of the Confederacy were already stretched to the limit for Charleston and the coast.

45.    Lieutenant General James Longstreet.

46.    Recall that Dr. Rivers was waiting to be court-martialed, but that the trial was postponed due to the absence of witnesses.

Apparently, he was returned to duty. No explanation is forth-coming.

47.     Brigadier General Thomas L. Clingman.

48.     Longstreet was, according to Robert E. Lee, "my old War Horse," the most dependable of the corps commanders in the Army of Northern Virginia.

49.     The sabre was donated by the family to the Jackson House, Lexington, Virginia, but is currently on loan to a museum in Greensboro, North Carolina.

50.     Lieutenant General Wade Hampton had commanded a cavalry brigade in Stuart's cavalry division, 2d Corps, Army of Northern Virginia since August 13, 1862. He would end the war as commanding officer of a Cavalry Corps of the Army of Northern Virginia.

51.     The first engagement of the Civil War took place at Fort Sumter on April 12, 1861. Stokes is referring to this fort, although he spells it "Sumpter."

52.     The fate of Dr. Rivers is not known.

53.     Captain Appleby commanded G Company; Captain Foster commanded H Company.

54.     Captain Barber commanded B Company.

55.     There is still no explanation concerning the disposition of Dr. Rivers' court-martial.

56.     Emanuel. His battalion consisted of Companies A, E, F, and I.

57.     Brigadier General  Micah Jenkins.

58.     No general officer of this name appears in the Index to the Compendium of *The War of Rebellion.*

59.     Major General George Edward Pickett.

60.     General Joseph Eggleston Johnston.

61. President Abraham Lincoln.

62. General Robert Edward Lee.

63. In writing of the raid to the Secretary of War, General Hunter reports: "This expedition is but the initial experiment of a system of incursions which will penetrate up all the inlets, creeks and rivers of this department, and to be used in transport steamers supplied with bulwarks of boiler iron, etc. . . . .Colonel Montgomery with his forces will repeat his incursions as rapidly as possible in different directions, injuring the enemy all he can and carrying away their slaves, thus rapidly filling up the South Carolina regiments in the departments, of which there are now four."

64. Battery Wagner on Morris Island, named in honor of Lieutenant Thomas M. Wagner, was one of the principal installations in the defense of Charleston. Writing of the battery, Brigadier General Ellison Capers says: "[It] mounted two heavy guns on the sea face, and some twelve or more, of lighter caliber, on the south and west faces. It was a strong earthwork, constructed of compact sand, upon which the heaviest projectiles produced little effect, with well-built traverses protecting the guns from the sea fire, high merlons, thoroughly protected magazine and bombproof, with a strong parapet on the north or gorge face, for the protection of the opening. The salients on the east and west were flanked by infantry and howitzer fire."

65. July 10, 1863.

66. A certain Dr. Glover.

67. To place or force into public service.

68. General Stokes' wife Eliza Jane.

69. Major General William B. Taliaferro, who had commanded a division in Jackson's Corps, Army of Northern Virginia, had been assigned to General Beauregard. He was ordered to take command on Morris Island on July 13, 1863.

70. R. S. Ripley. See note 6.

71. Brigadier General Thomas Jordan, Beauregard's chief of staff.

72.    Brigadier General N. G. Evans.

73.    There exists a state of confusion concerning exactly who were the noncombatants inhabiting the city. Major General Sam Jones, commanding Charleston, wrote Major General J. G. Foster that five generals and forty-five field grade officers, all prisoners of war, were housed with the civilians for safekeeping. In reply, General Foster wrote as follows: "Many months have passed since Major-General Gillmore, United States army, notified General Beauregard, then commanding at Charleston, that the city would be bombarded. This notice was given, that non-combatants might be removed and thus women and children be spared from harm. General Beauregard, in a communication to General Gillmore, dated August 22, 1863, informed him that the non-combatant population of Charleston would be removed with all possible celerity....That city is a depot for military supplies. It contains not merely arsenals, but also foundries and factories for the manufacture of munitions of war. In its shipyards several armed ironclads have already been completed, while others are still upon the stocks in course of construction. Its wharves and the banks of the rivers on both sides are lined with batteries. To destroy these means of continuing the war is therefore our object and duty. . . .I have forwarded your communication to the President, with the request that he will place in my custody an equal number of prisoners of the like grades, to be kept by me in positions exposed to the fire of your guns as long as you continue the course stated in your communication." (Ellison Capers, *Confederate Military History,* V.)

74.    General Stokes used this term to mean the passenger cars of the train.

75.    Fretworks.

76.    Metaphoric, short for thunderbolt, i.e., an artillery projectile, a shell.

77.    A wheeled support for the cannon.

78.    Major General J. F. Gilmer.

79.    See note 6.

80.  See note 72.

81.  See note 57.

82.  Charleston.

83.  Recall the previous engagement with the Tedinis on June 26, 1863.

84.  George Gordon Meade.

85.  July 1, 1863.

86.  A single-shot, lever-action, breechloading rifle named after Christian Sharps, the gunsmith who invented it.

87.  Major General Jeremy Francis Gilmer.

88.  These are never explained in any of the material extant. Rather, the letter serves only to demonstrate the "conflict of will" between Rutledge and Stokes.

89.  Major General M. C. Butler.

90.  General Stokes' brother-in-law, J. E. Boulware.

91.  Major General George Henry Thomas.

92.  Major General Ambrose Everett Burnside.

93.  Colonel Robert H. Anderson.

94.  C Company.

95.  Brigadier General Henry A. Wise, commanding the 6th Brigade, D. H. Hill's Division, Army of Northern Virginia, had been ordered with his command to Charleston to report to General Beauregard on September 11, 1863.

96.  Brigadier General B. H. Robertson.

97.  Major General William B. Taliaferro.

98.  Named in honor of Brigadier General John Bordenare Villepigue who died of a severe illness on November 9, 1862.

99.  Hardeeville.

100. A term that means trotting or running; modern, double time while marching.

101. A single-shot, muzzleloading rifle of .577 caliber, used in limited numbers by both sides in the Civil War.

102. Brigadier General A. H. Colquitt.

103. Lieutenant General A. P. Stewart.

104. Major General Joseph Wheeler.

105. See note 89.

106. General Stokes had been instructing his wife on how to sell the corn in his absence.

107. South of Jacksonville.

108. The other three were Colonel Charles J. Colcock's 3d Regiment, Lieutenant Colonel Robert J. Jeffords' 5th Regiment, and Colonel Hugh K. Aiken's 6th Regiment.

109. See note 71.

110. J. W. McCurry, regimental quartermaster.

111. Major General J. F. Gilmer.

112. Commanding officer of Company D.

113. See note 72.

114. John Dunovant, later Brigadier General in command of a cavalry brigade in General Butler's Division, Cavalry Corps, Army of Northern Virginia.

115. Benjamin Franklin Butler. On May 16, Beauregard attacked Butler's forces below Drewry's Bluff, driving him back to Bermuda Hundred Neck. General Grant says of this action: Butler was "as completely shut off from further operations directly against Richmond as if [he] had been in a bottle strongly corked. "

116. See note 14.

117.    Seven in number were required to ferry the command across the river.

118.    Lee needed to impose himself between Grant and Richmond. On May 21, he decided to move to Hanover Junction.

119.    General Stokes confused Stewart with Lieutenant General J. E. B. Stuart. The latter was mortally wounded in action on Telegraph Road, Yellow Tavern, on May 11, 1864, dying the following day.

120.    General Stokes' horse. Upon entering Confederate service, Marshal was appraised at $275.00.

121.    See letters, June 2, 1864.

122.    Atlee's.

123.    Pamunkey.

124.    This was Sheridan's cavalry. The infantry consisted of the 5th and 6th Corps.

125.    Fitzhugh Lee, Major General and nephew of Robert E., commanded a division in the Cavalry Corps, Army of Northern Virginia.

126.    Company K.

127.    Company B.

128.    The only confederate general officer named Williams was Brigadier General John S. He, however, was serving under General J. E. Johnston in Georgia on this date.

129.    Richmond.

130.    Gaines' Mill, June 26, 1862.

131.    On June 6, Grant finally raised a flag of truce, and the bodies were removed. This symbolized defeat. For whatever his reasons, Grant's three-day delay in deciding to do this cost him the lives of many who had been wounded. Some of them probably could have been saved if treated in time.

132. Major General George Brinton McClellan.

133. Isaac M. Liston, a horseholder.

134. June 9, 1863.

135. There was a Bethesda Church in the vicinity and a little more than a mile from Gaines' Mill, another, called Beulah Church.

136. Brigadier General August V. Kautz.

137. Brigadier General James H. Wilson.

138. Sometimes called "the engagement at Samaria Church."

139. See note 73.

140. This word is used in the sense of recovering or resting.

141. Lieutenant General Jubal A. Early.

142. See note 92.

143. General J. E. Johnston was relieved of command of the Department of Tennessee on July 18, 1864.

144. Company C.

145. Apparently a replacement for one of the original company commanders.

146. Lieutenant General John Bell Hood.

147. The bay was closed, but Mobile had not fallen.

148. Company D.

149. The crime appears to have been bestiality.

150. Variant of vedette: a mounted sentinel stationed in advance of pickets to watch an enemy and give notice of danger.

151. Culpeper.

152. Major General M. W. Gary.

153. Brigadier General A. G. Jenkins.

154. Brigadier General J. R. Chambliss, killed in action below Richmond on August 16, 1864.

155. Brigadier General P. M. B. Young.

156. Lieutenant General, Commanding 3d Corps, Army of Northern Virginia.

157. Although Brigadier General James Dearing was a cavalry officer in the Army of Northern Virginia, General Stokes is probably referring to his fellow South Carolinian, General Dunovant who was commanding Butler's Brigade at this time.

158. The following telegram from General Lee to Secretary of War James A. Seddon, dated August 26, 1864, demonstrates Lee's pleasure with the cavalry operations:

> GENL A. P. HILL ATTACKED THE ENEMY IN HIS ENTRENCHMENTS AT REAMS' STATION YESTERDAY EVENING, AND AT THE SECOND ASSAULT CARRIED HIS ENTIRE LINE. COOK'S & MACRAE'S NORTH CAROLINA BRIGADES, UNDER GENL HETH, AND LANE'S NORTH CAROLINA BRIGADE, OF WILCOX'S DIVISION, UNDER GENL CONNER, WITH PEGRAM'S ARTILLERY, COMPOSED THE ASSAULTING COLUMN. *ONE LINE OF BREAST WORKS WAS CARRIED BY THE CAVALRY UNDER GENL HAMPTON WITH GREAT GALLANTRY, WHO CONTRIBUTED LARGELY TO THE SUCCESS OF THE DAY.* [emphasis added] SEVEN (7) STAND OF COLORS, TWO THOUSAND PRISONERS, AND NINE PIECES OF ARTILLERY ARE IN OUR POSSESSION. THE LOSS OF THE ENEMY IN KILLED AND WOUNDED IS REPORTED TO BE HEAVY, OURS RELATIVELY SMALL. OUR PROFOUND GRATITUDE IS DUE TO THE GIVER OF ALL VICTORY, & OUR THANKS TO THE BRAVE MEN & OFFICERS ENGAGED.
>
> R. E. LEE

159.	Major General Thomas L. Rosser, commanding a brigade in Fitzhugh Lee's Division, Cavalry Corps, Army of Northern Virginia.

160.	I. McP. Gregory, Regimental Surgeon, 4th S. C. Cavalry.

161.	Brigadier General James Dearing was in W. F. Lee's Division.

162.	Since August 23, 1864, Lee had been recommending to Secretary of War Seddon and to President Davis that all work and agricultural details involving arms-bearing soldiers be revoked so that the number of combat troops could be increased.

163.	Thomas Preston Hampton.

164.	The election was held on November 6, 1864.

165.	Captain Henry McIver was to be placed in command of Company A.

166.	The Meherrin River.

167.	The Nottoway River.

168.	The Carolina Railroad.

169.	Both west of Branchville.

170.	North of Columbia on the Charlotte & S. C. Railroad.

171.	Salkehatchie.

172.	Under the command of General Alfred H. Terry, Fort Fisher had been captured and the port of Wilmington, the last port of the Confederacy, had been closed since January 15, 1865.

173.	Ted Jack is not identified. The latter is a neighbor known as Doctor.

174.	In a letter from General Lee to President Davis, dated February 9, 1865, he writes: ". . . .I beg leave to submit for your approval the following proposition: To allow me to proclaim by your authority a pardon to all deserters and absentees who will return to their regiments or companies within thirty days from the date of its publication at the headquarters of the military departments, with the assurance that this will be the last act of amnesty extended for such offenses. . . ." General Stokes had returned to his regiment before General Lee made this request and would therefore qualify for amnesty.

175.    Triple.

176.    Lieutenant General W. J. Hardee, in command of the Department of South Carolina, Georgia and Florida since October 5, 1864.

177.    The North Carolina Railroad.

178.    See note 155.

179.    Brigadier General Thomas M. Logan.

180.    On February 22, 1865, General J. E. Johnston was assigned to command of the Departments of Tennessee and Georgia, and South Carolina, Georgia and Florida.

# BIBLIOGRAPHY

## Unpublished Material

Service Record of William Stokes. Washington: Confederate Collection, National Archives.

## Books

Alfriend, Frank H. *The Life of Jefferson Davis.* Cincinnati and Chicago: Caxton Publishing House, 1868.

Amann, William Frayne (Ed.). *Personnel of the Civil War: The Confederate Armies, I.* New York: Thomas Yoseloff, 1961.

_____. *Personnel of the Civil War: The Union Armies, II.* New York: Thomas Yoseloff, 1961.

Brooks, U. R. *Butler and His Cavalry in the War of Secession: 1861-1865,* Columbia: The State Company, 1909.

Capers, Ellison. *Confederate Military History: South Carolina, V.* New York: Thomas Yoseloff, 1962.

Davis, William C. *Rebels & Yankees: The Commanders of the Civil War.* New York: Gallery Books, W. H. Smith Publishers, Inc., 1990.

Dowdey, Clifford (Ed.). *The Wartime Papers of R.E. Lee.* Boston: Little, Brown, and Company, 1961.

Evans, Clement A. (Ed.). *Confederate Military History, XII.* New York: Thomas Yoseloff, 1962.

Falls, Cyril (Ed.). *Great Military Battles.* London: The Hamlyn Publishing Group Limited, 1969.

Freeman, Douglas Southall. *R. E. Lee: A Biography, III.* New York: Charles Scribner's Sons, 1936.

Hotchkiss, Jed. *Confederate Military History: Virginia, III.* New York: Thomas Yoseloff, 1962.

Jarrell, Hampton M. *Wade Hampton and the Negro: The*

255

*Road Not Taken.* Columbia: University of South Carolina Press, 1949.

Stokes, (Rev.) John Lemarks. *A Genealogical Study: 1312-1903.* Yorkville, S. C.: Enquirer Press, 1903 (?).

*Webster's Biographical Dictionary.* Springfield, Mass.: G.& C. Merriam Company, Publishers, 1966.

*Webster's Geographical Dictionary.* Springfield, Mass.: G.& C. Merriam Company, Publishers, 1966.

# INDEX

257

258

259

261

263